To Dad
Love
Marlene
1973

SEVEN YEARS IN HANOI

Capt. Larry Chesley

SEVEN YEARS (IN HANOI)

A POW TELLS HIS STORY

by Capt. Larry Chesley

BOOKCRAFT INC.
SALT LAKE CITY, UTAH

Library of Congress Catalog Card Number: 73-84144

3rd Printing, 1973

LITHOGRAPHED IN U.S.A.

PUBLISHERS PRESS
SALT LAKE CITY, UTAH

TO MY COMRADES
Both those who returned and those who did not

CONTENTS

Preface ix

1 Shot Down 1

2 In Enemy Hands 7

3 The First Four Years 16

4 Day by Day 34

5 "Humane and Lenient Treatment" 50

6 Time the Essence 68

7 No Atheists in Hell Holes 82

8 Brotherhood Behind Bars 98

9 Toward the Light 109

10 Returned to Life 120

11 Local Boy Comes Home 132

12 Of Whitewash and Hogwash 142

13 God Bless America 152

PREFACE

I had never expected to write a book. But then neither had I expected to spend seven years as a prisoner of war in North Vietnam. After that experience I felt I had a story to tell.

I have no desire to write a treatise examining the Vietnam War or the part the POWs played in it. I leave such matters to others better qualified. My purpose in writing this book is to tell in a simple, understandable style, the story of my nearly seven years' captivity—the prison conditions, the treatment we received, and what we did and felt and thought through it all that helped us to hang on. While this is a personal account, I believe it is fairly typical of the longer-term prisoners.

In referring in this book to prisoners of war by name I use the ranks they held when captured. Many have of course been promoted since their release and other promotions will no doubt be forthcoming.

What I say in this book concerns only conditions in North Vietnamese prison camps. I cannot speak for those in South Vietnam, where American POWs were in the hands of the Viet Cong. As regards the circumstances of those men, which the evidence suggests may have been in some respects worse than ours in the North, I know only what I have read and heard.

I offer this book to the American people in appreciation for their evident concern for the POWs while we were away and in deep gratitude for the warm and wonderful welcome they gave us on our return.

Chapter 1

SHOT DOWN

April 16, 1966, began as just another ordinary day in Thailand. I got up at about one o'clock in the afternoon, had breakfast, then went down to our squadron building to a briefing.

We had a night mission. Night missions ran from 4:30 P.M. until 4:30 the next morning. Ours was to be the first takeoff, just before dark.

When I got to the briefing room, Lt. Hal Sheads, Lt. Col. Bob Conray and Major Sam Johnson were already there. Major Johnson and I were going to be flying the lead aircraft; the other two men, number two. As I walked into the room, Hal Sheads had some encouraging words, "Larry, I've picked an easy target for us tonight. There are no guns over there; it's just going to be a milk run."

"Thanks for the help, Hal," I replied.

Major Sam Johnson was an outstanding pilot, having flown with the Air Force acrobatic team, the Thunderbirds. It was my first flight with him, and I felt it to be an honor. I was anxious to return from this mission to write to my wife, my children and my parents, telling them I had just flown with a Thunderbird. I knew my family were very conscious of the feats of these outstanding flyers.

We went out to the aircraft and right away I should have known it was not going to be a good day. I had flown the night before, and the gun did not work then. In today's quick check it appeared to me that the gun had not been serviced, but the crew chief assured us it had been serviced and was in working order. We accepted this and went ahead—pre-flighted, walked around the plane making a visual check, checked the ordnance. Then we got in the plane and took off. It was 4:30 P.M.

For approximately thirty-five minutes we flew at a height of about fifty feet, arriving over the target around 5:05 P.M. We were flying in a two-ship formation—two F4-C fighter-bomber aircraft with two men in each. We always flew our night missions in two-ship formation so that we could watch out for each other. Major Johnson, a flight lead, was in charge of this mission.

The target was a cave on the east side of a large piece of karst[1] in southern North Vietnam, about thirty miles north of the DMZ (Demilitarized Zone). Having flown in on the west side of the karst, we intended to circle around and take a look at the target. But "milk run" or not, in our pass over the west side we were shot at. I punched my microphone button and told the second aircraft we were being shot at.

"Two," Major Johnson called, "can you roll in on the guns?"

"No," came the reply. "We're on the other side of the karst."

"All right," Major Johnson said, "we'll get them." We made a sweeping turn, diving at the ground and trying to fire our gun. It didn't work.

We were flying over a valley, going about 670 knots at around fifty feet. Suddenly we took a hit somewhere in the control system and the plane started to buck, as in a P.I.O. (Pilot-Induced Oscillation). Fortunately it started to pitch

---

[1] A kind of rock which looks something like coral and is spread over the Vietnam countryside.

upwards. If it had pitched downwards we would have been killed instantly by hitting the ground, whereas as it was we gained some altitude.

Within seconds we had been hit a second and a third time and the plane was on fire. We did not know about the fire until seven years later when, after we got back to the United States, our wing man told us that flame and smoke had been coming out of the aircraft.

With the plane now out of control, Major Johnson called out, "Get out! Get out!" I grasped the handle between my knees and pulled on it—but nothing happened. I tried again and once more nothing happened. I heard Major Johnson shout again, "Get out!" Then he ejected and I watched him go over the side of the aircraft and fall away. I was alone in the crippled plane.

On the top of my seat was a face curtain designed to protect the pilot's face from windblast on ejection. Pulling this curtain down and over the face activates the ejection mechanism, and this is the primary and better way to eject. But down between the pilot's knees is a ring hooked to the seat and known officially as the alternate ejection handle; and because his hands are already involved in that area with the stick and the throttle, the tendency is for the pilot to use this ejection method under emergency conditions. It was this handle I had pulled on without success.

Twisting in my seat, I now reached for the face curtain, but it was blowing in the breeze and in what pilots know as a negative G condition. There it was floating above me, and there was no way I could reach it. So I turned again in my seat, grabbed the handle once more, and gave it a mighty tug. This time it worked. I was ejected from the aircraft.

In the process I temporarily lost consciousness, and when I came to I was looking downward to see the ground rapidly coming up to meet me. Turning to look up, I could see my parachute was full. I tried to undo my seat kit, but it did not fall loose. I took off my oxygen mask. Then I looked toward heaven and said, "O God, please give JoDene strength to endure this hardship." It may seem strange to some, but at that moment I was more concerned for my wife than for myself.

It doesn't take long to fall a couple of thousand feet but it takes still less time for the mind to do the split-second reruns such as were now triggered by the thought about my wife. Crowding back came the scenes and recollections of the summer of 1960 when I met her; our marriage that fall; the rugged years when I was working my way through college with her uncomplaining cooperation; my rejoining the air force, this time for training as a pilot. As I fell through the air I couldn't help recalling that she hadn't liked the idea of my flying but had accepted it because that was what I wanted.

I worked hard at Officers Training School at Lackland, Texas, and managed to graduate as a Distinguished Military Graduate. Pilot training at Webb Air Force Base in Big Spring, Texas was difficult—I had a hard time learning to fly. But hard work and some hard praying got me the wings JoDene finally pinned on my chest. Survival School followed, then fighter training on the F-4C tactical fighter-bomber at Davis-Monthan Air Force Base in Tucson, Arizona, where I graduated as the outstanding pilot of my class.

Assigned to Eglin Air Force Base in Florida, after two months there I decided to volunteer for Vietnam—I would have to go at some time anyway and this was as good a time as any. JoDene accepted this reasoning, though she couldn't understand why I had to go just before Christmas. But leaving then meant that a man who had been flying combat missions for a year would be back with his loved ones for Christmas. I would be away only a year. I promised to write every day, even if the letter said only "I love you"—a promise I kept. I kissed my wife and two children goodbye on Pearl Harbor Day, December 7, 1965.

I didn't know exactly what combat was going to be like but I soon found out that it's a bit scary. On the second day I was in combat we lost one airplane, though fortunately both

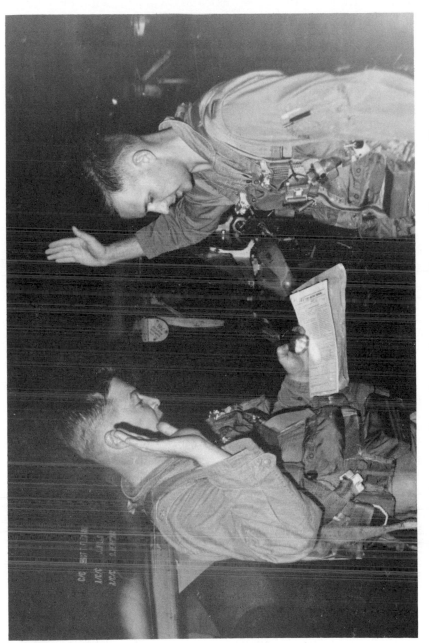

AUTHOR IN SURVIVAL GEAR, BEING SWORN IN AS REGULAR OFFICER IN THAILAND
AFTER NIGHT MISSION

men were picked up. The next day we lost another plane and, so far as we knew, both the occupants were killed; for it seemed that there was no way for anyone to get out of the plane. That really shook me, but I wouldn't let it get me down. I kept praying, asking for strength and guidance. And I wrote and told my wife that if I should be killed she was too young to remain a widow; that the children needed a good father; and that my only request was that she marry a good man who would take care of her and the children, take the children to church, and generally set them the right example in their religious life.

That thought had been either a momentary faltering of faith or a too-strict assessment of my human failings, for I sincerely believed I would return home in safety if I did my best to live right. There was comfort in this thought as I floated to earth. I had had lapses since making the original commitment to God, but I had tried to make amends for them. I had been praying regularly during the past few years, been active in the Church, and lived a clean and moral life.

The ground was not far away now. Clearly, there were many difficulties ahead. I had tried to keep close to the Lord when I *wasn't* in trouble. I felt that he would help me now that I *was*.

Chapter 2

IN ENEMY HANDS

I hit the ground feet first, then fell on my tailbone and was momentarily knocked unconscious. Quickly coming to, I stood up and took off the seat pack. Moments later I was surrounded by Vietnamese farm-workers. Frantically they set to work to take all I had. Not understanding how to work the zipper on my flying suit, they cut my clothes from me. When they had finished I had lost my clothing, revolver, survival kit, wristwatch—even my boots. I stood there in the field clad only in my underwear (garments) and my white socks.

I had had some experience with prayer and I knew that God listens. In my heart I now raised a short plea to him. "O God," I said, "I may have to walk a long way and I can't walk without my boots." About one minute later my boots were returned to me. I put them on and my captors started pulling me off across the field.

The ejection from the plane had cracked a vertebra and I was now in severe pain. Nevertheless they were making me run. Every step was pure agony. They took me several hundred yards across the countryside and put me in a hole dug in the ground. It was about three feet deep, six feet wide, and twelve feet long. Three men got in the hole with me and blindfolded me.

My captors could not speak my language nor I theirs, so I had no idea what was going on. But this was the kind of setup I had seen in the movies when someone was to be executed, and although I did not feel afraid to die, I thought that time might have come. But it turned out that they were only putting on a show for their people. They started bringing people to see me. While I could not see the visitors, so far as I could judge they were merely curious. None were hostile to me at this point.

I had parachuted into a farming-type area. There was no village—just a small cooperative, a storage area for grain. In an hour or so I was taken out of the hole and moved into a building. By this time I had been handed over to the military. In this building more people came to see me. Some of them pinched me, poked me with sticks, and generally harassed me a bit, though the guards tried to prevent this.

In this building I had a bad scare. It was around 9:00 P.M., about four hours after I had ejected, that I went into shock and the bottom part of my body became paralyzed. I could not move my legs. In my shocked condition I started to weep, because to me being crippled was worse than being dead. But after about thirty minutes the feeling began to come back in my legs and soon I recovered. I never had any more problem in this respect.

Soon I was on the move again. The guards and I walked until about midnight, when we came to a truck. In the back of the truck was Major Johnson. As I crawled on board, he asked, "Are you hurt?"

"Yes," I replied. "I hurt my back when I ejected. I see you have a broken arm."

"Yes, two of them," he responded.

I could now see that he had both arms in slings. He was still wearing his flight suit and boots.

The guards tied my arms together behind me with what looked like electrical wire and then tied my hands behind my back to the top of the truck, more or less suspending my body from them. It was an extremely painful position. Once again I called upon God. "O dear Lord," I said, "I can't travel very far this way." We had only gone about five miles when the knot at the top of the truck worked loose and I got my hands free. My arms were still tied behind me, but at least I was not hanging from them now. I was able to sit down in the truck. I even managed to loosen the wires on my arms.

We traveled most of that night until dawn the next morning, about 4:00 to 4:30 A.M., when the truck broke down. The guards took Sam and me off the truck over into a field by a bunker while they got the truck going again. We got back on the truck, traveled about another two hundred yards, and it broke down again. So they put Sam and me off at another bunker.

The terrain was extremely flat and one could see for miles around. It was plain that the guards were shaken by the knowledge that they were in an exposed position and that U.S. planes would be there at any time starting the morning bombings. They were so anxious to get away that when they got the truck going a second time they didn't even slow down when it passed Sam and me. They left us with a couple of guards to walk the last five miles or so to the village.

Before I had met up with Sam at the truck, a little old black-toothed woman in a hut I was in had given me a very overripe banana and a cup of warm milk. To me it was tasty and nourishing, and I was grateful for it. At one point too I had received some water. But Sam had had no food or drink since early afternoon of the previous day, and in any case his broken arms made his condition much worse than mine. By this time he was very sick. A couple of guards now stayed with him while one of them took me into the village. I assume they took the truck back later to get Sam. I didn't see him again until eight or nine days later.

In the village that day I stayed in a house. A Vietnamese-type sergeant came along with a "pointee-talkee"—someone who used a few words of English and lots of sign language. He asked such questions as whether I was hungry, thirsty, sick or injured. I said I was in pain with an injured back, and shortly after that a doctor came over. Apparently he wasn't smart enough to slip my underwear down, so he cut the back out of it to give me a shot. This eased the pain for a while. It was the only "treatment" I ever received for my injured back.

That night I was moved to another building about two miles away from the house, and it was at this building that I had my first interrogation. There were four Vietnamese on the tribunal. One of them said he was a Red Cross worker, and it was he who did the interpreting. He told me that the man asking questions was a general.

They asked me questions of military significance, such as what base I was from and what airplane I was flying. In reply I gave them my name, rank, service number, and date of birth—the only information I was required to give them under international law. They clearly were not happy about this, but to all their questions I returned this same answer.

After a while the general got up from his chair and came over towards me. Just as they do in the movies, he took off his revolver and put it on the table in front of me. The only light was coming from two little kerosene lanterns about three inches high, and in the dimly lit room I didn't see it coming when he hit me on the side of the head with his fist.

"It didn't hurt very bad anyway," I said. "I can take that for a long time."

At this he hit me again. Then he hit me a couple more times, but it really didn't hurt that badly. By this time he was getting rather angry and he kicked me. My arms were still tied behind my back and I was sitting in front of him. When he kicked me on the side of the head the kick didn't hurt so badly but it spun me around and I fell into what was about a ten-inch beam that put a big split in the front of my head.

They finally ended the interrogation and took me outside. Having tied me up with my arms tightly pulled together behind my back they threw me in an ant bed. The ants crawled all over me, though they didn't bite me. The mosquitos were feasting on me. I wondered exactly how long I was going to be able to take this kind of treatment.

After I had been on the ant bed for about two hours the guards came and loosened the cords on my arms somewhat and took me back into the building where I had been interrogated. This time I let my mind run away from me. Inside the building was a man with a little candle, a crucible, and some syringes and needles for giving shots. I thought perhaps they were going to give me a truth serum. I was told to sit down by the wall on a board, which I did. Meanwhile the man ignored me. Soon I was conjecturing that they were not preparing to give me a truth serum but to brand me with a prison number. Then I imagined all kinds of wild things.

Finally the man cleaned everything up and left. Soon I realized that he had just taken care of Major Johnson's arms.

The next day I had a personal guard. I was taken out of the house and put in a trench during the daytime, and this guard would beat me with a stick about eighteen inches long and maybe a quarter of an inch in diameter. Every time our aircraft flew over, or just whenever he felt like it, he would beat on me. He beat me across the back and shoulders but particularly on my right forearm, which now swelled to about twice its normal size.

At the end of the day the guard left. That night I prayed that God would take care of me and not let that guard come back the next day. God answered this prayer too—I had a different guard the next day and this one did not hurt me.

That day passed with no significant happenings, but my captors held another tribunal about ten o'clock the following morning. They asked the same questions as before and I gave them the same answers.

All the time, night and day, my arms had been tied behind my back with a wire cord. Now they tied them tightly together with a rope cord, took me out to a ditch about three feet deep, and threw me in it face downward. Then they repeatedly picked me up by my arms and rubbed me up and down on the rocks. There were quite a few spectators, and I concluded that they were putting on a display for their people to show that they had things well under control.

Because my right arm was so swollen, the skin tore off quite badly as they rubbed me up and down on the side of the ditch. It worked like sandpaper. I was left with a big sore about the size of a silver dollar. Later it healed down to about the size of a quarter. I still have the scar.

The next night they put me in the tightropes. This was their most effective way of torturing without leaving scars, and the North Vietnamese used it extensively in the early part of their torture sessions. They first wrap the victim's arms with cloth so that the ropes do not leave a scar. Perhaps they misjudged on this occasion, since I was wearing only short-sleeved underwear. At any rate, I still have a scar where the ropes cut into my left arm that night.

The principle is that cutting off the circulation to the victim's hands and lower arms causes him excruciating pain. I can vouch for this. With my feet tied together and my arms behind me, they put the ropes on my arms about eleven o'clock that night, cinching them until they almost tore my ribs apart from my sternum in the front. Then they made me lie on my back—in other words, lie on the ropes, which just tightened them all the more. The only way to get a little relief (small though it was) was to sit up. So I would sit up and the guards would come in and knock me back down. I would sit up again and they would come in and knock me back down again. I don't know how long this went on, but I know I was crying in pain and the guards were making fun of me. In my agony I didn't even know what they wanted of me. Actually they didn't ask me for anything this time. They were just punishing me for not answering their questions previously.

Finally, out of sheer exhaustion I just passed out. When I came to some hours later, my arms were completely dead. The guards came in and took the ropes off. I could use my hands after a day or two. It was several weeks before all the feeling came back in them.

Sam and I had arrived at the village on Sunday, April 17, and we left it on Monday the twenty-fifth, heading northward to Hanoi. I was still wearing only my underwear (minus part of the back, which the doctor had cut out), my socks, and my boots. It was cold, especially riding in the back of the truck at night, and as we went north it got colder still. The first night was unbelievable—it was so cold and my back was hurting so badly that I don't know how I made it.

I was never so happy to see a sunrise, because I knew that when the sun came up we would stop moving. I had learned that, to stay clear of U. S. aircraft, the North Vietnamese didn't move trucks during the daytime. So just after dawn they took us into a hut and put us on a mat. It was very hot during the day. I fanned Sam, who of course could not use his arms, and he slept for a while; then I slept for a while. So we passed away the day.

That night we moved on. As we walked out of the hut we found a crowd of two or three hundred people outside. We were both a little apprehensive at this—a crowd could be very unhealthy for us in our circumstances. But they just milled around us and didn't do us any harm. We got on the truck and it pulled away.

The next day we lived in a pagoda. We didn't travel that night but stayed in a church building. The following day there was an angry mob outside the building but we were protected by the guards.

The next night we were on our way again. When we reached the Vinh Ferry the truck drove onto it and the ferry got under way. We were about half-way across the river when I heard the boom-boom-boom of guns and immediately after that the sound of an airplane. "Oh boy!" I thought. "This

COL. (FORMERLY MAJOR) SAMUEL R. JOHNSON

is just going to be great—being shot up by our own planes." All the guards left the truck and got down on the ferry ready to jump over the side.

As it happened it was not a fighter plane but a photo-reconnaissance plane and the "booms" were the photo bomb cartridges that provide the light for the camera. It was a great relief to discover this.

When the ferry reached the other side the truck started up the road and about ten minutes later another photo-plane came skimming over Highway 1 right over our heads, taking our picture again. Once more all the North Vietnamese abandoned Sam and me.

That night we stayed at a camp in the city of Vinh. Here Sam and I were split up again, as we had been back in the other camp. We were here for a few days.

On May 5 we heard a lot of shooting in Vinh. Later the guard came in and gave me the sign of a parachute floating down, indicating that they had captured another prisoner. About two hours later Major Johnson was brought to the room I was in. "I think they got another flyer," I said.

"I do too," he replied. "That's probably why they brought me here—they're taking him over to where I was staying."

This was confirmed for us when we boarded the truck again at about ten o'clock the following night. Our new traveling companion was Navy Lt. John Heilig, who had been flying an RF-8 photo-plane when he was shot down.

We pulled into Hanoi at around 11:00 A.M. the next day after about twelve hours on the road. The twelve foot rock-and-cement wall surrounding the huge prison compound looked fittingly ominous with its surmounting barbed wire. The truck pulled up outside the big iron gates, the guards kicked us off the truck, and we walked inside. The gates closed noisily behind us. We were in the notorious "Hanoi Hilton."

This is where I was destined to spend much of the next seven years.

Chapter 3

THE FIRST FOUR YEARS

The name *Hanoi Hilton* is of course the Americans' nickname for the major prison compound in Hanoi. The Vietnamese are more realistic. Their name for it is *Hoa Lo,* which means "hell hole."

Built by the French, it is a huge compound roughly rectangular in shape, the long wall measuring perhaps two hundred yards. It is divided into several sections, each of which we POWs referred to as a camp. One camp we knew as Little Vegas, its rooms inevitably being dubbed by Las Vegas casino names — Desert Inn, Stardust, Golden Nugget, The Mint, and The Thunderbird. Another camp we called Camp Unity. Two other camps, Heartbreak Hotel and New-Guy Village, were the primary areas for initial interrogations.

Major Johnson and Lt. Heilig went to Heartbreak Hotel, while I was taken to New-Guy Village. I had my initial interrogation there, then was sent to my cell. I was still clad only in my underwear, socks, and boots.

I was "solo" in this cell. It was about twelve feet by six feet. The walls were of a rough plaster and colored a dirty white. Butting to each of the long walls was a hardwood bed with the head fixed to the six-foot wall opposite the door, leaving about a two-foot aisle between the beds. Each bunk had a thin rush mat for a "mattress."

The bunks were fitted with leg irons—wooden, rather sharp-edged cut-outs for the legs with a hinged iron portion on top that could be locked in place. About 3½ feet from the floor, they extended the width of the room across the foot of both beds, so that a prisoner had to climb over or duck under them to get to or from his bedspace. Leg irons were one of the punishments given for infractions of the prison regulations. Typically a term of leg-iron punishment might be a month—with the hands handcuffed behind the prisoner's back night and day. He would be released during that time only to get his food and eat it twice each twenty-four hours. If he were lucky he would be able to relieve himself at those times.

The height of the room was between fifteen and eighteen feet. A half-oval window about six feet high began about eight feet from the floor. It had no glass—no room I was ever in in prison had any glass in the window frames—but its iron bars were as strong as ever. When the outside shutters were open, the eye took in a view of a couple of feet of the rock and cement wall surrounding Hanoi Hilton, with its broken-glass top and the three parallel wires above that carrying electric current.

The room was devoid of furniture—unless you could use that description for the bucket in the corner.

That first afternoon I heard somebody softly singing the song "Besame Mucho." That is, the tune was there but the words were different. The words said: "My name is Lt. Col. Robinson Risner, American fighter pilot. If you hear me, cough."

I knew that Col. Risner was a prisoner. What I didn't know was whether this was some trick of the North Vietnamese, and since I was trying to keep ahead of them I wouldn't respond. The voice continued singing the song, repeating the colonel's name and asking me to cough. But still I wouldn't cough.

After a few minutes, the song started to give me instructions. "Don't wear your socks," it said. "You'll need them in the wintertime."

"Hmm!" I said to myself, "they'll probably steal my socks if I take them off."

Now the voice sang me a few other helpful instructions. Then it started singing again, "If you're air force, cough."

Finally I gave in and coughed. That was what the colonel had been waiting for—just to get acknowledgement that I was there, that it really was a prisoner in the next cell. Now he started asking me questions and I answered him in code—one cough for yes, two coughs for no, three coughs for "I don't know." Pretty soon I just jumped up and held on to the window ledge, and we started talking back and forth. He was in the same position in his room. The precautions were necessary to minimize the possibility of discovery—we were separated to preclude communication, and talking to each other was therefore punishable.

The colonel began talking about other prisoners. "Do you know Captain Jon Reynolds?"

I answered no.

"Do you know Airman Art Black?"

No again.

"Well, do you know Captain Bob Jeffery?"

In my excitement my voice rose. "Bob Jeffery? He's dead. He was in my squadron."

"Sh!" the colonel cautioned. "Keep your voice down. No, Bob's here."

"Well, how about George Mimms?"

"I don't think George made it," the colonel replied.

Bob Jeffery had been shot down four months before I was, on December 20, 1965. That was only four days after we had arrived in Thailand, and in those four days we had lost two airplanes, Bob's being one of them. I was very glad to discover that he was alive. Later I found out he was LDS.

Col. Risner now gave me some more information on camps, senior officers, and so forth, and cautioned me again not to talk too loudly because we'd be in trouble if we were caught.

The next day I was issued with prison clothes and the guards took away my underwear. It was absolutely filthy after twenty-one days of rolling in dirty trucks and on dirty floors, and the guard would not even touch it with his hands. He picked it up on a stick and carried it out of the room. I assume he burned it.

I had to go through some minor interrogations that week. In one of them I was asked to write down the names of my squadron mates on a paper I took back to my cell. I put the pencil and paper on the second bed in the cell and left them there. The guard who brought my meals could of course see that I had written nothing.

From Col. Risner I was learning something of my captors' methods for obtaining information from the prisoners, and I now began trying to prepare myself mentally to be tortured to write the required names. At nighttime, the day after I received the paper, I heard people coming along the hall. This was it, I thought.

The door opened and three guards came in. One carried a bamboo step-ladder. The three now proceeded to change the low-powered lightbulb in the cell, which had burned out. As they left, one of them took the paper and pencil.

I never heard any more about my failure to write as requested. Perhaps that try-on was one of the tactics used to test the new prisoner's temperament and get some initial measure of his resistance.

By Thursday I had developed a boil about the size of a golf ball in my left armpit. It was extremely painful. I talked to Col. Risner about it. "Well, they don't give us too much medical treatment around here," he said, "but it'll take care of itself. I think you'll find it will be okay within a day or two." I hoped he was right. I asked him to pray for me and he said he would.

The next time we talked we got onto the subject of religion. When we had finished I asked him if he had ever heard of the Mormon Church. "Yes," he replied, "I've heard of it."

"Colonel Risner," I said, "I would like you to make me a promise."

"Okay, Larry, what it it?"

"I want you to promise me that when we get out of here you'll look up the Mormon missionaries and learn about our Church."

"Okay, Larry," he responded, "I'll make that promise to you."

That made my day. I have a tremendous respect for Col. Risner. He's one of the greatest guys I've ever known.

At the end of that week, about 6:30 P.M. on Saturday, I was lying on my bunk when my boil burst, giving me relief from its pain. This came after much praying on my part— and on Col. Risner's too, I'm sure. I cleaned my armpit up as best I could with a dirty rag I had.

There are many prison compounds in North Vietnam besides Hanoi Hilton, and that Saturday night I was moved to one we called Camp America or the Zoo. It is across town in the southwest part of Hanoi. Here again I was to live alone.

There were ten cells in the building I was in. At first only five of them were filled and these were all on the same side. Mine was the end cell. Major Al Brunstrom was in the one next to me, and as he began giving me information I found out that Lt. Jim Ray was next to him, then Capt. Bob Purcell, then Capt. Jon Reynolds. After we had lived there for some days, prisoners were brought into four of the cells on the other side of the building. This made a total of nine prisoners in the building, all living solo.

In that building we started a practice that I continued throughout the rest of my stay in prison. At the first meal of the day, when every man had his food, we would give a signal through the building. Each man would then recite the Twenty-Third Psalm and ask a blessing on the food.

On Sundays too we had a special practice. There's nothing like prisoner-of-war life in a communist country to emphasize the importance of religion and patriotism in one's life, and we made love of God and our country the paramount theme and an anchor to our souls throughout those years. Each Sunday we would pass the signal around, then each man would kneel in his separate room, offer a prayer, and recite the Twenty-Third Psalm or the Lord's Prayer. Then he would pledge allegiance to the flag.

We were all aware of the words of Jesus, "Where two or three are gathered together in my name, there am I in the midst of them." He was indeed with us in these little services. To others, each of us might have seemed alone, but to us the separating walls were insignificant for those few minutes on Sunday. We were together in spirit.

Prison life tended to sharpen appreciation generally. I remember that first Sunday in that building. At about two o'clock in the afternoon the camp radio started playing classical piano music—Chopin. It was beautiful. I hadn't realized until then how much I liked classical music. Being alone and listening to good music seemed to be an inspiring combination. I asked Al Brunstrom if we got that kind of music every day, and he said yes. But he must have misunderstood the question. The following Sunday we got the radio program of classical music, but we rarely got it again during our prison stay.

The first U.S. bombing raid on Hanoi took place on June 29, 1966, and that night some of the prisoners, including me, were moved from Camp America in Hanoi to a country camp we knew as the Briarpatch. It's out in the country in the rocks, and a very poor camp it is. Once again I was solo.

On July 6 of that year the Vietnamese staged the infamous Hanoi March. From various prison camps they gathered, as I recall, fifty-six U.S. prisoners, handcuffed them together two by two, and marched them down the main street of Hanoi. My roommates-to-be, Navy Lt j.g. Bill Tschudy and Air Force Lt. Al Brudno, led the march. Later they told me the details.

To enhance and record the spectacle, big trucks carrying floodlights and cameras kept pace with the marchers. The road was lined with people. At first they just stood and watched, but as the march got under way a man started yelling into the microphone, stirring up the onlookers. They began shouting "Bow your heads! Bow your heads!"—at least, phonetically that is what they were trying to say, though it hardly sounded like the English words.

The Americans would not bow their heads—they held them high and looked straight ahead. Aroused by the man with the microphone, the onlookers took on the character of a mob as they pushed in among the prisoners, grabbing their necks to force their heads down. The prisoners got punched and kicked, and hit by flying bottles and rocks. As the crowd surged in, the march became a riot, each pair of the prisoners becoming separated from the other marchers. One man would be holding up his buddy, who had just been hit in the stomach or kicked in the groin and was unable to walk, and the next moment it would be switched and the other guy would be injured. It was very fortunate that no one was killed in this shambles.

The next day the camp commander's voice came across the camp radio: "The Vietnamese people demanded that we bring you to Hanoi," he said, "that they may see you and punish you; and what the people demand, we do." This of course was nonsense. The people don't demand anything in that country—they do what they are told to do. Three days later the English-language paper, the *Vietnam Courier*, said: "When scores of dozens of American prisoners were being brought somewhere to be interrogated, spontaneously a crowd arose to greet them." They lied about the circumstances, the number of prisoners, and the crowd. There was no spontaneous reaction—the crowd were told to be there and were manipulated while they were there. It was obvious to the marchers that the responses of the crowd were being turned on and off as with a switch.

At that time there was talk of war crimes, of bringing the prisoners to trial in North Vietnam. We heard that President Johnson had given an ultimatum that if any man were tried, North Vietnam would be totally destroyed by U.S. air power. Whether this was true or not, the Vietnamese backed off from the war trials idea.

After the march some of the men were tortured to write statements the North Vietnamese could use for propaganda. Others were called in just for interrogation and asked what they thought of the march. Most of the prisoners responded that they had seen the animals of Vietnam in the streets that night. Of course, that didn't make the interrogators very happy; but our men weren't very happy either, being black and blue from the bad beating the mob had given them.

I did not take part in the march. I don't know if this was because I was sick or because my name had not been released as a prisoner of war and they didn't want it to be released. Everyone in the march was bound to be identified, of course, so with a few exceptions the Vietnamese only put in the march the men whose names they had released. My name was not officially released until April of 1970, four years after I was shot down.

On July 11, another group of prisoners was moved to Briarpatch, and at this time the man who had been living solo next to me was moved into my cell with me. This was Jim Ray, an air force lieutenant. A few years younger than I and a bachelor, Jim was from eastern Texas, a graduate of Texas A & M, where he was president of the student union. He had been Top Gun in his F-105 fighter-bomber class at Nelis AFB. In addition to having this kind of background of achievement, he was just an all-around good guy. His coming was a partial answer to prayer, for I prayed constantly in prison for two things—to have a good roommate I could get along with, and to have a roommate who could teach me a foreign language. When Jim moved in with me it was an answer to my first prayer.

We got along well, especially considering the close quarters. A Baptist, Jim knew a lot of scriptures, and we talked about religion a great deal. I told him all I knew about my church, The Church of Jesus Christ of Latter-day Saints, and we discussed different points of doctrine. I have a great affection for Jim, and I like to hope that some day he will consider seriously the things I told him about my religion.

We moved around in Briarpatch from building to building and ended up in Echo Hut. I was still in a cell with Jim. In this four-room building there were seven of us, and we enjoyed each other's company very much. Al Brudno was the one who lived alone. We talked to and taught each other as best we could through the walls. We had a lot of fun, but we had to be careful not to get caught communicating between rooms, for then we would have been in deep trouble.

Inevitably, some prisoners were caught and punished. The punishment at this time consisted of being confined to a hole in the room. We had a bomb shelter in each room, a hole just dug out of the dirt. The holes contained sharp rocks, they often contained a pool of stagnant water, and they were always full of mosquitoes. The punishment at this time for communicating between rooms was to live in that hole for three months with the hands tied or cuffed behind the back, without a mosquito net, and without any blankets to keep you warm. It was a gruesome punishment. Captains Bob Lilly, Dick Bolstad and George McKnight spent some time in there—how long, I don't remember; the prison authorities shortened the three-month sentence in their cases.

Capt. (Formerly Lt.) James E. Ray
at Press Conference

That Christmas we got a special meal I'll never forget. Turkeys were brought into the camp, and we each got a little piece of turkey meat with our rice. We had soup. And we had lettuce and carrots for the first time since I had been a prisoner.

Before this, in October of 1966, it was time for another torture session—the first I was involved in while in prison. As I shall indicate later, it left my feet in a torn and painful condition, so that when in mid-December the feet began to hurt again I thought this was a recurrence of the effects of that session. Actually it turned out to be beriberi.

At first this new difficulty was principally a nocturnal problem. When I lay down to go to sleep at night my feet would start aching. I would have to get up and walk for thirty or forty minutes and then they would feel okay for a while. By late December they were hurting almost all the time. I had asked to see a doctor but the prison authorities wouldn't bring one. Pretty soon the prisoners started talking about it in the building, and then we found out that several of the men's feet hurt. It turned out that all these men had basically the same symptoms. The feet would heat up and hurt; they would feel as if they were being twisted, being wound up like a rubber band. I thought sometimes that the intense, unrelieved pain would send me crazy. We were not allowed out for exercise, but we found that if we walked in our rooms or ran in place it helped ease the pain, so we did this.

Things got progressively worse all through January, the feet hurting more and more until finally I just had to be walking or running almost all the time. I was now at the lowest ebb in my prison career, the only point at which I was ever really depressed. By this time about 50 percent of the Briarpatch prisoners had this problem. Jim was one of those who didn't have it, and he did his best to encourage me.

On February 3, 1967, all the Briarpatch prisoners moved back to Little Vegas at the Hanoi Hilton. I needed that. Even though I was still in the same pain, different surroundings and new things seemed to give me a fresh start in life. Here we were given a few epsom-salt foot baths, and these would relieve the pain for me for about ten minutes.

February merged into March, and things were no better. Although we were in the city, where we usually got bread, we were still instead getting rice with our not very good soup. I was losing weight. I had gone into prison at about 160 pounds, but by March 1967 I weighed only about 100 pounds —a loss of approximately 60 pounds. Most of that had come off in the previous three months. My health was bad and getting worse. I could sleep only twenty or thirty minutes out of a twenty-four-hour period, and that was when sheer exhaustion overcame the pain. It was a very cold winter and we did not have enough clothes or blankets to keep us warm. Yet my feet were uncovered the whole winter because they felt as if they were on fire. They were so hot that they burned the hair off my leg halfway to the knee.

During this period I was lying on my bed one day feeling more dead than alive when my roommate Jim Ray, in his concern for me, started yelling for a doctor. The guard came in and started beating on me. At this, Jim jumped out of his bed, picked the guard up, and threw him out of the room. The guard was furious. He took off his rubber-sandal shoe and was going to hit Jim with it, but Jim stood up to him and said: "If you hit me with that I'm going to take it away from you and beat the hell out of you." The guard didn't understand English, but he got the message. He left.

Pretty soon he was back with an entourage. I was afraid for Jim, because just about the worst thing a prisoner of war can do is to hit a guard. At survival training at Stead Air Force Base in Reno, Nevada, we had been told emphatically, "Don't ever hit a guard!" Yet Jim had done that for me because he wouldn't let that guard beat on me.

At that time they didn't do anything to Jim, but later an English-speaking North Vietnamese came and told him he would be punished. A few days later was Tet, the Vietnamese New Year, and Jim was punished that day. The authorities knew that the guard was in the wrong but they had to save face, so they "punished" Jim. His punishment was that he had to stand in the corner for one minute.

They got even with him about two weeks later, however, when he was caught talking to another room. He was taken to interrogation, and when they asked him what he had said he told them that he had a very sick roommate. "He needs a doctor very badly and you won't give him one," Jim told them, "and I was asking if any of the other men knew how to take care of his foot problem." Jim got put in leg irons for fourteen days for that.

It did a little good though. They took me to the doctor. All he did was give me motor-skill tests on my legs, and when he found out that I had all the proper reflexes he sent me back to my room the same night. They didn't really do anything for me until about March 18, when they finally moved me with Jim from the Desert Inn to the Golden Nugget, a sick bay area in Little Vegas. For thirty days I received shots, including Vitamin B1, B2, and B12. In addition I got "extra" food, which in those days was unusual. That extra food was as follows: First, I received bread when all the other men received rice; and second, when we got pig fat the guards would cut the minute pieces of lean meat from all the other prisoners' portions and give it to me, making a total of perhaps a heaped tablespoonful. I began to feel better, I started gaining back some weight, and my health generally improved. But beriberi had run my body down so badly during those bad months that I was sick most of the time that I was in prison. I caught any disease or sickness that came along.

During those very sick days from January through about the last of March the pain was so intense that I could think of nothing but pain. Even thoughts of my wife and children whom I loved so much, and whom normally I thought about all the time, were ousted by the demon pain. Those were very trying times. In all, I was in pain for between four and five months, and after I started getting my health back my feet still hurt quite badly for several more years. Even today they are not completely normal.

In May of 1967, Jim Ray and I received two new roommates, Navy Lt. j.g. Bill Tschudy and Al Brudno, first lieutenant in the air force. These were very fine men. A former marine, Bill Tschudy came from Highland, Illinois, near St. Louis. He had been his senior class president at high school, then a graduate of SMU where, though a "Yank," he had been popular enough to become president of his fraternity. Bostonian Al Brudno, a graduate of MIT, where he had been the ROTC commander, was brilliant in his knowledge of the sciences, and later would prove to be an extremely competent instructor in our forty-eight-man room. Being shot down cut short his aspirations to be an astronaut.

Bill was an Episcopalian. Al, who was Jewish, had been reading the Book of Mormon (given to him by an LDS man, his best friend) during the period before he was shot down. Now we had in the room a Mormon, a Baptist, a Jew, and an Episcopalian, but religious differences were insignificant to us. We loved each other in the Christian sense, we helped each other, we taught each other, and we tried to keep ourselves busy, especially our minds.

Later that summer of 1967 we were split up again and Jim and I were put in another building, still together in a cell. In the last part of July and the first part of August we went through another torture session. Then our captors moved us to the workers' quarters right next to the power plant. They did this in the hope that it would persuade the U.S. not to bomb it. It was bombed, however. This is the time when I thought I might be injured. When the bombs fell the window shutters were closed, the doors were barred, and the overpressure in the room was so great that the window and the door were blown off the building. A sagging string that ran from one end of the room to the other snapped when the walls buckled.

After that experience I believe the North Vietnamese were afraid we might be killed. At any rate, they moved us

Lt. j.g. William M. Tschudy (Left) and Lt. Alan Brudno Leading the Hanoi March July 6, 1966.

to a camp we called the School. At one time it had been a French school for the Vietnamese.

In October of 1967 we were all moved back to the Hanoi Hilton, where I was put in a cell in Little Vegas. When the guard opened the door the POW already there greeted me with a big smile which revealed a gap where, shortly after he parachuted down, part of a front tooth had been knocked out by the rifle barrel being used to push a gag in his mouth. The smile and Navy Lt. Gerald Coffee's warm handclasp told me I had again been blessed in the allocation of a roommate.

Jerry is one of the most outstanding people I have met, either in prison or elsewhere. A former student body president of a large high school in California, he had been quarterback on the school football team. He had been on the ski team for UCLA, where he graduated with an art degree. And he had graduated number one in his pre-flight class, where he was a battalion commander, and also in his pilot training class.

Jerry had been in captivity about two months longer than I. He had a broken arm when he landed, but that didn't deter his captors from tying his hands together over his head and suspending him from a tree by his hands. He was wearing a ring when he left the plane, and the broken arm, the callous treatment of the guards, and the pressure of the ring caused the finger to swell to an enormous size. When he sought some relief from his captors, instead of sawing or breaking off the ring, they took him to a room, threw a cloth over his head, and cut three deep incisions in his finger to relieve the pressure of blood. This rendered the finger permanently bent and useless. The broken arm too was set in a way that produced a deformity.

The cell I was in with Jerry gave the most cramped conditions I was ever in. It was about nine feet long and forty-two inches wide. Butting to one of the long walls, a two-bunk hardwood bed extended from the hallway wall to within two or three feet of the exterior wall, leaving about one foot of space to move in between the long edge of the

—*Official Photo*

CMDR. (FORMERLY LT.) GERALD L. COFFEE

bed and the opposite wall. If I extended my arm as I stood at the head of the bed with my shoulder touching one wall, my fingertips touched the other wall. The leg irons on each bed in this cell were locked and unlocked from the outside hallway.

Jerry and I got on very well together in the thirteen months we lived together—October 1967 to November 1968. This was probably my most spiritual year in prison. Twice a day I prayed diligently seeking help, guidance, enlightment, and health, and Jerry did the same—each praying privately. In that period we talked a lot about religion and I taught Jerry, who is a Catholic, what I knew about the gospel. I remember the night I left Jerry. I said, "Well, Jerry, you may not be a Mormon but I know you can never quite be a Catholic now." He just laughed.

In November of 1968 I left Jerry and moved to Camp Hope, near the city of Son Tay, about thirty miles northwest of Hanoi. This time there were seven of us in the room, and it turned out to be an enjoyable situation, even though Camp Hope was a poor camp. In February and March of 1969 a strange and wonderful thing happened—several of us received packages from home. It was the first thing we had heard or received from home during our prison life. Even though my parents did not yet know whether I was alive or dead, I now received a package from them. It was a good feeling to know that our loved ones were still back there and had prepared those packages with so much loving care.

Throughout 1969 I was quite sick, a sickness generally associated with stomach problems. I had a hard time eating and I never gained much weight. Now and then, about once every three months, the camp authorities would give me special food—perhaps sweet milk, or a couple of tablespoons of extra meat.

The year 1969 was sort of a nondescript year. Somehow, time just passed. In the fall of that year another purge came, another torture session, and it swept through the camp. The last man in the purge was being tormented in October. Then one day they just took him back to his room and that was the end of the torture session. They didn't often do that— they didn't stop before they got what they wanted.

It was in that month that conditions began to improve. It had been five years before this, August 1964, that the first prisoner in North Vietnam was shot down—Lt. j.g. Everett Alvarez. Food now improved somewhat; we got dental treatment on a wide basis for the first time; and we got outside a little more to get some sunshine—a couple of times a week.

The best part of all was that by the end of 1969 we began to feel a little more secure. We were apparently not going to be tortured any more. Now we just had to hang on. With God's help I'd done that in the tougher conditions of the nearly four previous years. With the same help I could hang on in the less difficult times ahead.

Chapter 4

DAY BY DAY

The encyclopedia describes Vietnam as a hot, humid, tropical country. In the summer, "hot and humid" is an understatement for North Vietnam. In the winter it's a deceptive term. Normal winter temperatures range probably from forty degrees at night to sixty in the daytime. In January and February, the coldest months, if it gets unusually cold these figures can drop to around thirty-two and fifty respectively. Several nights in my experience we found out from the camp authorities that the temperature had dropped to freezing point. Even if the temperature is not quite that low it gets cold in bed with only a thin rush mat between the sleeper and the hardwood or concrete bed and only two light cotton blankets to cover him. Needless to say, there was absolutely no heating in any of the camps.

In Chapter 3 I described a couple of typical small cells or rooms in Hanoi Hilton. The rooms varied in size, of course, some being intended for larger numbers of prisoners. A four-man cell would be perhaps 6½ feet wide and 9 feet long, with a hardwood double bunkbed on each side and a small aisle, eighteen inches to two feet wide, between the two tiers of bunks. Rather close quarters, even when you got used to it.

There were much larger rooms in some sections of the compound, as in Camp Unity, and after November 1970 we lived in them in larger groups and in less unpleasant conditions. But the prison authorities were particularly proud of the smaller rooms, as in Little Vegas. These were of North Vietnamese design and construction, a modification of the larger rooms bequeathed to them by the French. They had a definite purpose.

The North Vietnamese split the sixty-feet by twenty-four-feet rooms in Little Vegas into eight very small rooms with hallways between the rooms. This meant that the only wall common to any two rooms was the exterior one. They made these structural changes for the deliberate purpose of preventing us from communicating between rooms. Actually it didn't work. We communicated anyway. When they found this out, their former pride in their creative conception and execution changed to irritation and annoyance, for it made useless the considerable time, energy and money they had expended on this project.

There were several features to our covert communication system. Some prisoners had a personal song—"The Yellow Rose of Texas," for example. When you heard this being whistled or hummed or sung, you knew that So-and-So was out washing his clothes, or whatever else he was doing. This told you, for instance, that he was still around, still in this particular camp.

The most effective means of communicating was a tap code—tapping on the wall of the cell. To the best of my knowledge, Captain "Smitty" Harris initiated the system in the prison, having learned it as a Boy Scout. Its basis was a five-by-five block of letters. It took hard work and a lot of time (of which we had plenty) but by this means we passed and received a lot of information, both "intelligence" type and educational.

Besides the tapping on walls, the code could be used in other media—by a man shaking out his wet laundry, for example. A broom in a POW's hands could be another useful signaling device. On occasions when we swept leaves in the courtyards, or swept out the hallways a few times a month,

if enough rooms were represented by the sweepers it was possible to pass information through the entire camp even though
we could not speak to other POWs.

In the early days, before the prison authorities learned
of its significance, the five-by-five block was brought to the
attention of new prisoners in several ways. It was written on
some of the cell walls. In one of the interrogating rooms it
actually had been scratched onto a table, presumably by some
enterprising POW who improved upon his time and opportunity when left alone to ponder his "crimes" or during a
torture session. Underneath the letter block was the injunc-
tion, "All prisoners learn this." How much good effect this
had on the new prisoner as he sat there suspicious of everything in sight is of course questionable.

When the prison authorities found out what was going
on they had all physical traces of the code removed. They
knew we were tapping, and they knew about the code. They
would make us "break it up" when we were communicating
by strokes of a broom. What they could not do was stop us
tapping on walls. It was to prevent this that they had built
their masterpiece at Little Vegas. It failed in its main purpose, though it did have the advantage from their point of
view of keeping us in small groups and thus making communication difficult.

Not only did they try to cut us off from talking to other
prisoners not in our own room, but they went to all lengths
to prevent us from seeing them. As an example, occasionally
they would take all the prisoners living in one building to a
propaganda movie depicting the glorious feats of the Viet
Cong in winning the war in South Vietnam. It would be
shown at night and we prisoners would sit on the ground to
watch it. Blankets would be strung up in such a way as to
allow us to see the film yet preclude us from seeing or communicating with anyone not in our own cell. To enforce this,
guards would be strategically placed among us. Needless to
say, we did manage to communicate through the blankets.

To the warped minds of our captors there were reasons for their efforts to prevent us from seeing and hearing each other, but even allowing for their determination to control all our input of information, to us it seemed they had an obsession about it. Much of the time they kept the window shutters closed. In any event, in many of the buildings I was in the base of the windows was about eight feet from the floor, so a person would have to climb and crawl into the window to see anything outside. Theoretically one man could stand on another's shoulders to look out, so they blocked the windows with mats. This restricted the air flow and added to our discomfort, especially in the hot and humid summer. The design of the buildings made for poor circulation of air anyway.

The courtyard at Hanoi Hilton was sectioned off with tar-paper partitions nine or ten feet high so that when our men went to and from the "bath" area they couldn't be seen by other POWs. We found ways to get around this—for example, whenever possible we would make a small peephole in the tar-paper. At Camp Hope, where the bath area was differently situated, we would make our peephole in a door or a window shutter, concealing it with a nail or dirt when not in use. Stimulated by the enemy's elaborate plans to the contrary, we made it a habit of watching each other going to and from the bath area, getting food, or pulling weeds in the sun on the rare occasion when we had this privilege. We had a lot of fun doing this and got a lot of information which we duly passed around from room to room.

Keeping the rooms clean was a trick in itself. We tried hard, but it was very difficult because the prison authorities wouldn't give us things to clean them with. Sometimes we would just go out when it was our bathing time and, without their permission, take some of the water we might have bathed with and scrub our floors and our beds down. Sometimes it was impossible even to get a broom to sweep our floors, for when the one allocated wore out (and they wore out very quickly) we would have a hard time getting another.

For the most part the clothes we wore were black pajamas, though they varied in color from time to time. At first they were a greenish color which turned into sort of a silver tan as they faded. Next we had pajamas with purple and grey stripes. Later we had black pajamas. Those were the most common, and most of us were wearing them up to the day we were released. At first the pajamas must have been made for Vietnamese, the tallest of whom are 5 foot 1 or so. Later the North Vietnamese used 260-pound Sergeant Bill Robinson as a model. The resultant pajamas were pretty baggy on my 5-foot-8-inch, 130-pound frame.

Our standard issue per man, for outer clothing, was two pairs of long pants and two long shirts. The shirts tied with draw-strings and the pants were held up by the same method. None of the clothing had any pockets. We also each received two short-sleeved T-shirts and two pairs of boxer shorts. All this clothing was made from the same material—a sort of heavy and stiff cotton material. In the winter we each received a sweatshirt in addition. For winter in those early years too some luckier prisoners got socks. In the later years we all received socks in the winter. On our feet we wore Ho Chi Minh-type sandals made out of old tires.

After the first 2½ years or so, when our clothes wore out we received new ones. Up to that time we just wore what we had, trying to take as good care of it as we could to prevent it from falling apart completely. It was almost impossible to get a needle to repair the clothes, so once they started to go they went pretty fast. Later the Vietnamese did start letting us have needles and thread for short periods of time to take care of our clothes.

Each of us had a very small towel measuring about two feet by one foot. There was no washcloth. We each had a toothbrush and a tube of toothpaste. The toothpaste had to last two months. Usually the toothbrushes wouldn't last that long. They were very cheaply made of brittle plastic and broke easily. It was a great godsend when, after the end of 1969, we received toothbrushes and toothpaste from home, but that improvement lasted only until December of 1970. At that point the Vietnamese took all our American things away from us.

As well as the items I have mentioned, we each had one mosquito net, two blankets, and a small rush mat. We used the mat to sleep on and to pile our few things on during the day, to keep them as clean as possible.

A tin cup to drink from completed each man's personal gear. In the earlier period we had water jugs which were filled up twice each day. They were small jugs, but for me this was enough water. In those early days some of the bigger men were hurting during the summer for lack of water. Later the situation improved—after 1970 the drinking water came in about five-gallon containers, and then we almost never ran out.

Ironically, the only hot water we ever had in North Vietnam was drinking water. To make it safe for drinking it was always boiled first, and when we got it, it was usually hot. As to water for personal cleanliness, we "bathed" in cold water all the time, summer and winter, using a lye soap similar to what grandma used for washing the clothes. It was very strong to the skin at first but we became accustomed to it with time. One bar of soap had to last forty-five days in the earlier stages, but this was later cut back to thirty days.

For the first eighteen months or so up to about the end of 1967, any "bathing" was sporadic. We might get to wash ourselves one day, then nine days later, then five days after that, then thirteen days later. We might be allowed to shave once every week or two. After 1967, for two years or so we usually "bathed" three times a week. Later this changed to nearly every day. Starting in 1970, we got an improved supply of water for bathing and washing clothes. We never knew the reason for this improvement but conjectured that the North Vietnamese had built larger reservoirs to supply the camps.

The bath areas in the early days were dirty and rundown.

After I had been a prisoner for two to three years the guards did whitewash those areas, and this improved things a little.

We used cold water and our lye soap in shaving. At first we were allowed to shave only once a week, but later it changed to twice a week. In the early days we were given one blade for the entire camp to shave with; later, one blade for 3 men; and toward the end, one side of a blade for each man. Sometimes we felt that weekly, monthly, or even yearly shaves would have been preferable because the blades were so poor that they tore up our faces. But during the summer the beard would make us sweat and itch and it was nice to be able to shave—when the shave was over, that is. We got haircuts about every five or six weeks, generally from the guards, though sometimes they would let us cut each other's hair.

The heat in the summer was unbearable, and during that season many prisoners were absolutely covered with heat rash all the time, not being able to keep themselves cool or properly clean. Most of my roommates were afflicted like this. In this respect I was luckier than most. The heat did not bother me as badly and I had heat rash only once in all the time I was in prison.

I should perhaps clarify some terms. First, *bath area*. In Camp Unity at the Hanoi Hilton, for instance, this consisted of a small cubicle with an asphalt-type floor, a drain for the water to run away, and a cistern of cold water (not drinking water) allocated to the room for that day's ablutions. The prisoners' rooms were built around a compound of roughly rectangular shape, each room having an immediately adjoining bath area inside the compound. Use of the areas was staggered so that no two adjoining bath areas were occupied simultaneously.

At other camps the physical arrangements were sometimes different. For example, at Camp Hope near Son Tay the bath area was a separate, detached, concrete-floor cubicle in the center of the compound. We took turns using it room by room. (But for our peephole, we still would not have seen prisoners from any room but our own.) In other respects the bathing facilities were the same in all the camps I was in.

Second, *bathe*. We scooped water from the cistern with our drinking cup and threw it over the body. After soaping, we rinsed in the same way. Then we dried off as best we could on the minuscule towel.

We washed all our clothes and our towel by similar arrangements—cold water and lye soap. Depending on the camp we were in, we either lay the laundry on the ground to dry or hung it on wires or cords strung outside the bath area. Needless to say, by American standards the results were somewhat less than satisfactory. Clothing odors were a fact of life. Towel odors in particular were unspeakably bad.

In the early days the water supply was unstable, and occasionally there would be an unexpected difficulty or even an emergency. An example is the occasion when we ran out of water at Little Vegas during the summer. The conditions were bad in this camp anyway, and not being able to wash made them terrible. At this point the Vietnamese dug "wells" right in the courtyard and we would dip water out of these holes to bathe with. It was practically surface sewage water. This was a grim experience, only just better than not bathing at all.

By a stroke of luck I once had an unusual and heartening experience in the small outside cubicle that was our bath area at Little Vegas. It was November 20, 1967. Several of us were standing out in our respective bath areas when an air raid siren went off, and when the guards came to take everybody back to their cells they somehow overlooked my roommate Jerry Coffee and myself. As we watched, a flight of four F-105 fighter-bombers flew in echelon formation right over the city of Hanoi.

With flack and surface-to-air missiles all around them they were calmly flying along as if coming back to the home air base. They came in at about thirteen thousand feet, rolled in on the target, then peeled off as they might have done in a practice break. Having dropped their bombs, they did not come back up but scooted out over the city at low altitude and high speed to make way for a second and then a third group, each of which did the same thing. In my circumstances this couldn't fail to be an inspiring sight—an expression of the courage and discipline of flyers who knew that some of their number would find themselves one day in prison with us; a symbol of the air force's dedication to duty in prosecuting the war against a communist enemy I knew to be inhuman and barbarous; and a reminder of the great country I had been blessed to be born in.

Despite the numerous SAM missiles fired, not one of the planes was touched by enemy fire. Of course, that night Hanoi claimed nine shot down. They just couldn't have planes fly over Hanoi without claiming several shot down.

There were many unpleasant things to get used to in prison, one of them being the constant presence in the room of the bucket we used to urinate and defecate in in most of the camps. We were allowed to empty these buckets either every day or every other day. In the former case we had only a constant odor; in the latter, a stench. Both the appearance and the smell made them offensive. One of the men I lived with had diarrhea for almost the entire time we were there, and he had to defecate six or seven times a day whatever else was going on in the room at the time. You don't have to have a very active imagination to visualize the situation, but it's just another one of the more minor problems we got used to.

Of course, we could get some fun sometimes out of almost any kind of situation, even emptying those buckets. At Camp America a couple of the guys were doing this one day, a bucket in each hand, less intent on the buckets than on picking up note drops for other buildings. These had been written on toilet paper in lead from pencils stolen from guards, then left by another room under some bricks by the open pit which served for sewage disposal. The guard always accompanied the men only so far—there was nowhere significant they could go, anyway—and for a short while they were out of his sight.

They put the buckets down by the pit and began searching for the notes.

Through their peephole the room that had left the notes watched the two men's antics as they located the notes then triumphantly held them aloft in acknowledgement to their comrades before one of them hid the notes in his clothing. Having accomplished the major mission they picked up the buckets and began making their way back. They had gone a dozen or so paces before their faces reflected the realization that there was something wrong—they had not emptied the buckets. By the time they had rectified this and got out of sight again the men behind the peephole were convulsed in uncontrollable laughter.

The prison authorities certainly didn't help in the matter of room odors. In the country camps, most of the time during the day they left the shutters closed, winter and summer, thus decreasing the already poor ventilation. Generally they would open them about 6:00 P.M. and close them again at 5:00 A.M., and since there was no other means of light in the small cells we virtually lived all the time in the dark. In Hanoi Hilton, mats at the windows restricted light and air circulation, but we did have one low-power electric light per room burning day and night.

In the country camps we would have to feel our way around at night, and in this respect we became somewhat like blind men in that we could move about our rooms easily just by feeling and touching. One night I was going over to the bucket, not knowing that one of my friendly roommates had left the lid off. Feeling around for the bucket with my hand, I couldn't find it—until I finally felt the liquid inside it. My roommates got a good laugh about this.

We were nearly always hungry in prison, and when you're hungry one of the things you talk about the most is food. We would sit there on our beds and talk about food. We would describe in mouthwatering detail different types of dishes our wives made that we liked so much. We would list the kinds of food we would like to have right then. We would discuss the subject of food from all angles. Then at the end of such a conversation we would almost invariably ask each other: "Well now, if you could just have one thing to eat, what would you like to have?" And just as invariably the answer would be a hamburger and a milkshake. I guess no food seemed more American and reminiscent of home than a hamburger and a milkshake.

For each prisoner—not as a personal issue but for general use—there was a spoon, a metal bowl and a metal plate. We never had a knife or fork. Meals would be brought in pails by the guards, who ladled them out into our individual bowls or plates when we lived in the smaller rooms. After November 1970, in the forty-eight-man room, they left the pails for us to serve ourselves. As with everything else, we washed our dishes with cold water and lye soap. At times we were issued with extra soap for this purpose.

The North Vietnamese gave us food in amounts sufficient to keep us alive. The variety was something else again. From April until about October we got pumpkin soup—almost every day, twice a day. We would also get a side dish twice a day. Sometimes this consisted of squared pumpkin. That's pumpkin soup with pumpkin on the side dish. The other "main" dish was a bowl of soup made with kohlrabi, or sewer greens, as we called it. Sometimes the side dish would have one piece of pig fat about ¼-inch thick and an inch square, but we rarely got even this much meat. We did now and then get some unplanned "protein," however, resulting from the unsanitary methods of preparation—like the occasional caterpillar, and the chicken head, complete with feathers and one eyeball, that I once found in my soup.

The food preparers went one better than that on one occasion at Camp America. The guards duly came with the pails for the afternoon meal, ladled out the food, and left. The next morning, through our peephole we discovered that bread was being taken to the next room. Soon the communication system was at work. We asked the question: "Hey! How come you guys are getting bread?"

Maybe we shouldn't have asked. The question came back: "Did you enjoy your soup last night?"

"It was no worse than usual," we replied.

"Good," the next room responded. "We didn't get anything to eat last night. When the pail came in here and the guard was ladling out from the bottom of the bucket, he pulled out a dead rat."

Generally speaking we got bread if we were in a city and rice if we were in the country; though the rule wasn't hard and fast because sometimes we got rice in the city and at one of the country camps we got bread. Most of us preferred bread.

As I mentioned earlier, I lost sixty pounds in weight, most of it in three to four months. I then gained thirty pounds back over a four-year period. At that point I had put on two inches in my waist even though I was thirty pounds lighter. This was because, though the food was unappetizing and nutritionally poor, its bulk stretched our stomachs.

Many times there was no salt in the food, and that makes even good food hard to eat. This situation improved somewhat as time went on, until towards the end, in the big room, we actually had salt in containers

Up to about the end of 1969 we received food only twice a day, about 10:00 A.M. and about 3:00 P.M. Since the meals contained little or no meat content they digested in two or three hours. On this diet, around nine or ten o'clock every night a man began to get pretty hungry, and as the night wore on it got worse. Hunger stretched itself through the nights and into the first few daylight hours. When we were getting bread with our meals, we would frequently save a little bread from the three o'clock meal and eat it around nine in the evening to help stave off the extreme hunger pangs a bit longer.

It is impossible for a person living under normal circumstances in the United States to really understand what it means to be undernourished and hungry. It's not like deliberately being on a diet. It doesn't mean just going without food for two or three days. It means going for days and weeks and months seeing your body deteriorate, feeling yourself become steadily weaker. It means lying in bed at night with a blanket on you trying to keep warm and feeling the fire go out inside of you just as if you had turned off the thermostat. It cannot be described—only experienced.

Actually it was not as bad for me as for many of the other prisoners because I'm built relatively small. The big men were the worst sufferers from inadequate food intake. I recall that at Christmas 1969 several in our room were too sick to eat more than a little food. One man, a big fellow who had just moved in with us, ate all the food they had left. When he finished he told us it was the first time he had felt full since being taken prisoner some four years previously.

My experience with hunger has impelled me to one iron resolve—with God's help I intend never to be hungry again. I am going to set up a personal food storage program to take care of my family and myself.

I thought about this subject a tremendous amount in prison and also talked to my fellow prisoners about it. For years the Church leaders have been urging us to take this action—to store in our homes enough food and other necessities to last our families for at least a year. It's time we started taking the counsel of these prophetic leaders seriously. There in prison I convenanted with God that when I was released I would rapidly implement a complete storage program.

I have all kinds of experience to go on. It's not only food I missed in prison but an adequate supply of "little" things— things as simple as salt, soap, toothpaste, toothbrushes, toilet paper, scissors, fingernail clippers, needle and thread. I'm going to store some sweet things for taste treats, not only for children but for adults—how we craved them in Vietnam! I'm going to store coal for heating and cooking. In prison I designed ways to have pumps available so that I could dig a well and get water. I'll be sure to have sleeping bags, which are useful to keep warm in if there is no fuel for heating, yet are standard items for summer outdoor use in normal times. And I'll store warm clothes for use when the home can't be heated. One day perhaps I'll write a small book on what I've learned about the things we need to store.

Since returning to civilization I've seen little children again and heard babies cry. And I've said to myself, "What would that mother do if the baby kept crying and she had nothing to give him to eat?" It's the same with older infants and children—I don't want ever to hear any children in my family cry from cold or hunger. I might say that this was a topic of discussion with my roommates in prison, some of whom could see the need to set up such a program for their own families.

The physical health of the prisoners varied. Some of us seemed almost never to be sick, whereas others, when they got down, couldn't get back up, couldn't seem to get their strength back. I was in the latter category. I was sick most of the seven years. The four or five months when I had beri-beri were probably the worst torture I had in prison because it was sustained over such a long period of time. Other people had toothache for years, and what a torture that can be! A toothache is something you just can't run away from. Stomach problems were another health difficulty. So was asthma, and several people nearly died because of it. They did not receive the treatment they needed. The North Vietnamese would not let us receive medicine from home that would help us.

A thing that plagued the prisoners was diarrhea. Someone in the room almost always had it, and though you might go for three or four weeks without it, it would always catch up with you again. This probably was the most common malady among all the prisoners.

The North Vietnamese took away the glasses of any prisoner who arrived wearing them. Families sent glasses to the prisoners but our captors would not give them to us. As we got off the plane at Clark Airfield in the Philippines, the commentator said: "Notice, none of them are wearing glasses." Yet probably 50 percent of the returned prisoners ended up wearing glasses after they got back to the U.S.A. because their eyes had deteriorated in prison or because they wore glasses before they got there—or both.

When I received the news on July 25, 1972, that my wife had divorced me and remarried, the emotional shock brought on some serious physical developments. At that time I was at a prison camp in the north not far from the Chinese border. My condition scared the camp authorities, and in August they sent me back to Hanoi Hilton for a month for special care and treatment. This was really a joke, if a grim one, because the "special treatment" was worse treatment than I had been receiving at the camp in the north, except that in Hanoi I was getting shots each day. But however that may be, with the Lord's blessing I recovered. I went back to the camp in the north in September, and from that time on I was not sick again—except for one short bout with a stomach problem, probably caused by the excitement, just as we were released. It just seems that the Lord was preparing me to come home. He was giving me back my strength. At the time of writing (April 1973) I have not been sick since leaving Vietnam.

This chapter on prison conditions would give an incomplete picture if I didn't say something about the conditions under which we moved from prison to prison; for if the camps themselves were unpleasant, the method of transportation from one to the other was horrendous. We always moved at night. We would roll all our gear up in our mats and carry them with us. A blindfold was put on each of us before we left the old cell block, and when we got in the trucks our hands were handcuffed behind us. We traveled that way, blindfolded and handcuffed, packed like animals in the back of a truck which carried also a fifty-gallon tank of gas, breathing the fumes from the poor-combustion engine as we rattled over the rough, bumpy roads.

The worst journey of my life was that between Hanoi and the camp near the Chinese border. When we POWs went to that northern camp in May 1972 we traveled in exactly the conditions I describe above, except that on this journey we were not blindfolded all the time. This grueling ride over rough roads lasted about twenty-eight hours. Since about the end of 1966 my back has not bothered me to any great extent except when I have had to ride for long periods of time without being able to lie down—and you can't lie down when your hands are handcuffed behind your back. The back certainly got a workout on that ride.

When we got to the new camp everyone was saying, "The only thing that will make that ride seem good going back is that we will know we will be going home." But as I mentioned, I took sick and was sent back to Hanoi. Another fellow and myself made the return journey in the back of one of those trucks. When we reached Hanoi we were so beaten up by the rough ride that the guards had to lift us off the truck. A month later we went back again to the northern camp. So we got that little round trip twice.

On the final journey back to Hanoi in January 1973, there were twenty-four of us in a truck that should have held about ten. These conditions were bearable only because we knew that at long last we were on our way home. That thought overpowered every other.

Chapter 5

"HUMANE AND LENIENT TREATMENT"

The North Vietnamese have all along insisted that they gave the American POWs "humane and lenient treatment." There is, of course, always room for difference of interpretation and definition. The Vietnamese background is different from ours. No doubt, too, they would have given Vietnamese nationals the same kind of prison treatment they gave us if the circumstances had been the same—probably worse, since they would not have had to answer to the U.S. government or a world conscience. So perhaps to them *humane* and *lenient* are relative terms. To us they were not, and we saw nothing humane or lenient in the way they treated us.

That is not to say that we did not recognize the need for rules and regulations in the prisons, or that one would expect prison conditions to be pleasant, especially in a backward country. The North Vietnamese naturally had to keep order and maintain their control over us as prisoners. But that is not a valid excuse for the severe rules and restrictions they placed upon us or the harsh punishments they inflicted for infractions of their regulations. The basic reason for all this was to make us cowed, to break our spirit. That they did not succeed is, I feel, a tribute not only to our covert system of communication (at once a veritable life-saver to us POWs and a source of great annoyance and frustration to our captors) but also to the strong U.S. military discipline we managed to maintain and the self-discipline which this encouraged.

Though I have used the term *guard* loosely, in the prison we distinguished between two kinds of guards—the turnkey and the guard. When we left the cell to go to the bath area, to an interrogation, or to get food, and when we returned, it was the turnkey who locked and unlocked the cell door. He was not armed. The guards proper were armed with a rifle and patroled the prison grounds generally. They also were the ones who actually inflicted the tortures in the torture sessions.

Many of the Vietnamese officers in the prison chain of command were holdovers from the days of French control. Having worked for the French in the prison in those days, they spoke French, and that is presumably why they also spoke English. One or two of them seemed to be reasonably intelligent as regards intellect and reasoning power; the rest of them were pretty low-grade. They were all party men, dutiful servants of their communist overlords.

By and large the guards were even lower grade than the officers. Some of the things our peepholes revealed one or two of them doing were unspeakably crude and obscene. As to their reactions to us POWs, the concensus among the prisoners was that to all intents and purposes they were computerized robots doing what they were programmed to do. I have previously spoken of people being turned on and off as with a switch. This is exactly the impression the guards gave. They would go along for a while performing their tasks in sort of an average manner with no particular sign of either hostility or friendliness. Then suddenly one morning they would be mean and hostile in all their actions and attitudes. This might go on for some time before there was another change, then for a day or two they would smile and attempt to be friendly. This was not an individual thing—they all changed at the same time and kept it up together. It was as if they were told each morning what attitude they were to display to the prisoners that day, and indeed there can hardly have been any other explanation.

Of the many guards I encountered, only one seemed to have any inner doubts or glimmerings of conscience over what he was doing. Most of us prisoners felt that he was doing what he did because he was a good soldier and therefore obeyed orders, but that he didn't always enjoy what he was having to do. None of the others seemed to have any qualms about their activities in the prison.

I have been asked whether we did any converting among the guards, whether we changed their concepts in any way. A lot of fellows tried, but personally I don't think we had the least success. It's very difficult to convert someone who is determined his beliefs are right and yours are wrong, especially when he has no objective basis of evaluation. We couldn't convert them any more than they could convert us.

As one would expect in this modern age, in prison we were subjected to what we might call a psychological warfare. First, as I have explained, our captors tried to prevent us from communicating among ourselves. In this way they hoped to deprive us of all sources of information except their own. If they had been successful, we would have known nothing about any other prisoners; we would have received no information about the progress of the war or life in America or any other information from the outside world which was brought in by new prisoners; we would have been unable to warn each other when a "quiz" (interrogation) was in progress, or brief each other on answers already given under torture; and so on. In short, all our information input would have been under Vietnamese control.

From the speakers in our room we would hear the program Voice of Vietnam as broadcast by "Hanoi Hannah," but we were reading so much between the lines that our captors eventually quit giving us that program. We also got local programs, material the camp authorities obtained from Vietnam news agencies and read to us over the speakers—about thirty to forty-five minutes' worth a couple of times a day over short periods. This too was quite sporadic. Generally the news on these programs was about the great North Vietnamese victories "over the air war of destruction" and the wonderful Viet Cong victories in the South (which we knew they weren't having); or something that some high-powered U.S. senator or other American celebrity had said condemning the war or otherwise making a comment our captors could turn to their advantage.

While we improved our covert communication system as time passed, the North Vietnamese similarly improved their methods of propaganda. The propaganda programs coming across the camp radio were easily recognized, and no one paid any attention to them in the early days—in any case they were broadcast to the accompaniment of Vietnamese music, which in general is not particularly attractive to the American ear. Later the Vietnamese got smarter and started playing American music at the beginning of the program. Naturally we would listen to this. When they had our attention somewhat they would turn on their propaganda.

It is difficult to say what effect these programs had on us. We knew the material was all slanted to the communist viewpoint but we always hoped we could pick out some truth in the error and lies they were perpetrating. With no independent source to check on, it was difficult to make an exact determination between truth and lies. The broadcasts made sure we learned negative things about news in America—the strikes, the riots, the demonstrations for peace, the figures for increased crime, the earthquakes and other natural disasters, and anything which could have the effect of depressing us or, as they hoped, converting us. It seemed to make them happy to give that kind of information about America.

Their line of reasoning about the war was the only one we heard except what we could talk about among ourselves. It was the Nazi regime under Joseph Goebbels, the German propaganda minister during World War II, which popularized the concept that if you tell people a lie big enough long enough and often enough they come to believe it; and I can readily see how, when the truth is withheld from the listeners, this could be so. I even noticed that sometimes when we prisoners got into discussions on the war or the situation in South Vietnam or some other related subject, now and again men would unintentionally use arguments put out by the North Vietnamese. I even caught myself doing it sometimes. These arguments had intruded upon us subconsciously it seems because we had heard them reiterated so many times. That was the extent of our acceptance however. None of the prisoners whom I knew experienced a change of view or conviction as a result of the Vietnamese propaganda broadcasts.

If those broadcasts were not successful, the *Vietnam Courier* was certainly not going to be. The *Courier* was a Vietnamese newspaper written in English which we received at irregular intervals—every month or two. The strictly party line written in the sterile political style and without the softening preface of pleasant music had no power to persuade. Nevertheless many of us read it so that we could find out, by reading between the lines, what was really going on in the world. Here again the North Vietnamese stimulated us to read it by starving us of all other kinds of literature. Until about the last month or two communist propaganda material (either North Vietnamese, Chinese or Russian in origin) was the only literature we had to read during our entire prison stay.

One way and another, mainly in bits and pieces, we managed to get quite a bit of information, some of it even from the North Vietnamese. Naturally the prison authorities told us about the three American astronauts being burned to death, because that was a disaster and would make us feel bad. Eventually, too, they told us about the deaths of President Eisenhower, General DeGaulle, and other dignitaries.

We found out about the death of Walt Disney from a new prisoner. It was a sad and touching moment. Remembering the imaginative, entertaining and always wholesome movies associated with his name, we felt almost as if a part of America had passed away.

It was about February of 1970 when we discovered that America had landed men on the moon. On the radio program called the Voice of Vietnam, Hanoi Hanna read a letter taken from an American soldier after the Viet Cong had killed him. In that letter, which he was writing to his mother, he said that he didn't have to ask Neil Armstrong what the craters of the moon looked like because he could see them in South Vietnam. When we heard this our room just about went crazy with excitement, knowing now that Neil Armstrong knew what the craters of the moon looked like. By this time things were easing a little in prison and we were able to press the Vietnamese somewhat into telling us when America had landed the first men on the moon. Finally they gave us this information.

The POWs could not understand Vietnamese and our captors did not try to teach us it. As a matter of deliberate policy we would not try to pick it up; thus maintaining our separate status, making no concessions that would even hint of collaboration with the enemy, and forcing our captors to address us in English. Nevertheless it was amazing what we could learn just by listening to the Vietnamese radio. For example, in 1968 my roommate and I deduced from the outpourings of the speakers outside our window that the Tet offensive had started. We knew that the Viet Cong "fight song," so to speak, was "Liberate the South," and whenever the radio played it almost continually over a short period we knew there was something big going on in the war. On this occasion we noticed that for about a week every third or fourth song coming over that radio was "Liberate the South," and we concluded that they were trying to stir up the people's ardor for a big push that was going on. Sure enough, later we learned that the Tet offensive had been in progress then.

On another occasion, while I was at Camp Hope, one day the Vietnamese radio not only played the communist "Internationale" a lot but also played over and over again a popular song (which I thought had a rather pretty tune) about Ho Chi Minh. Six of us in our seven-man room agreed that this betokened Ho Chi Minh's death. A few days later we found out that he had indeed died.

Prison life in any country has its strains and stresses, and there were a good many already built into the prison conditions for POWs in North Vietnam. Apparently these were not adequate "to make the punishment fit the crime," in the eyes of the North Vietnamese. They had to add cruel and even barbaric physical treatment. From the POW point of view this treatment was meted out for two purposes: As punishment for breaking the harsh prison regulations, and as deliberate torture.

I have already mentioned the punishments of the leg irons and the mosquito-filled hole. Another device consisted of U-shaped clamps put around the ankles to which a sixty-pound iron bar was attached behind the leg. It was bad enough in this position, but to make it worse the guards sometimes reversed the clamps and put the bar on the front of the ankles so that it cut into the bone. A typical place for this punishment was the bath area, where a man would be left in this situation for several days.

Our captors used some methods either for punishment or for torture as the mood took them. One of these was to make a man kneel on a concrete floor for days and nights without relief, during which time his knees would swell up like balloons. An alternative was to make a person stand continually while his legs would swell to twice their normal size. Refinements of these basic methods included making the victim hold his hands above the head, or putting rocks or an iron bar under his knees as he kneeled, thus inducing greater pain and cutting off the blood circulation. The guards would not stay all the time, so we would try to relax in our position or steal a few minutes' sleep whenever we could. When the guards came in and caught us doing this they would slap us around with their hands, rubber hoses, or tire-soled sandals. To them, beatings were in any case a valid method either of punishment or persuasion, and many a prisoner was in fact beaten senseless.

It would appear that torture is an instrument of policy in North Vietnam, standard practices being used by authorities throughout the country. I had experienced torture methods shortly after my initial capture, before reaching the prison at Hanoi. I was to experience a good deal more in prison.

On the matter of torture there was apparently a difference of philosophy as between tormentor and victim that was reflected in their respective usages of the term. To us the issue was that we were being asked to do something contrary to our will and conscience. When we refused we were coerced by physical pain and torment until we gave in and did what we had originally refused to do. By all the definitions we knew of usage and history, in the English language the methods and purposes of the coercion taken together were properly described as torture.

The prison authorities, on the other hand, used the word *torture* only when denying that they had tortured us. Their "philosophical" position, if I understand it aright, was: (1) They had set up prison regulations; (2) Any prisoner who broke a regulation deserved and would receive punishment; (3) One regulation was that the prisoners were to obey every order of the prison authorities; (4) A prisoner who refused to write a particular statement when ordered to was disobeying an order and thus breaking a prison regulation. Thus when a POW refused to write as directed he was punished until he repented—not tortured, but punished. The proof of his "repentance" (and our interrogators actually used the word *repent* in this connection) was, in their words, "action by your practical deeds"—the prisoner would now obey the original order and the punishment for disobedience would cease.

This Vietnamese distinction was apparently too subtle for our Western minds to properly comprehend, so we POWs stubbornly called the procedure torture. I continue to use that term throughout this book.

The initial interrogation was concerned principally with eliciting military information. When we were in prison, however, the emphasis was on making us write propaganda statements, anti-war statements, admissions that we were criminals, messages condemning the policy of the U.S. government, and so on. Our captors also wanted to get biographical information from each man which they could similarly use for their own ends. They tortured us too to tape-record "good treatment" statements, which we assumed they would release to the world after we got home.

The interrogation sessions came at irregular intervals and we never knew who would be the first to go. The first one or two had no warning, but after that we passed the word around through our communication system, briefing others on what questions to expect and what answers had been given so that as far as possible we could all keep our answers consistent. We did not feel obligated to tell our tormentors the truth if it could be avoided, though each of us knew full well that the North Vietnamese could get from a prisoner anything they wanted if they just applied enough pressure.

When a torture session was in progress it was pretty hard to relax in your cell. No one knew who would be next. The jingle of the turnkey's keys in the hall outside a man's cell would give him a knot in the stomach and bring on a cold sweat—in fact, I suspect the North Vietnamese deliberately used this jingling to strike fear into our hearts. If your door opened, there stood the turnkey with an armed guard and you were led away to an interrogation room. There one of the English-speaking prison officers would tell you what it was they wanted this time.

It is difficult at best to fathom the workings of another person's mind, even if he has the same basic background of culture and education as oneself. I am certainly not qualified to analyze the North Vietnamese mind or that of any one individual there. The premise on which they worked, as they expressed it to us, was that they had the right and obligation to teach us the truth. If we would not accept what they said, force was a correct instrument of coercion. In the words of the camp commander, "We have the right to force you to recognize the truth."

With their Vietnamese and communist background, their poor education, and their lack of appreciation for what we knew as freedom, they apparently could not understand that we had minds of our own and that we really approved of and gloried in the right to dissent which was our birthright as Americans. Apparently too they could not or would not understand that a person cannot be forced to believe something, however much he may be constrained to give verbal agreement. Their applying force to us just turned us against them all the more. It is conceivable that if they had treated us in a humane way they would have had better success in influencing at least some of us. As it was they failed completely.

That failure frustrated them. One of the camp officers summed up their frustrations on this score by saying, "Some of you intentionally try to misunderstand the camp authorities." As to the reactions of those camp authorities as individuals, my feeling is that some of them more or less rationalized their way into a sincere belief that they were doing the right thing in trying to force our cooperation. I am quite certain on the other hand that some of them took a sadistic pleasure in what they were doing to us.

Once in the interrogation room, the prisoner would be asked to write whatever kind of statement the North Vietnamese were currently requiring. Routinely this request met with refusal. There would be an attempt to persuade the prisoner by "reasoning" and argument, including the threat that his refusal to comply would constitute breaking a prison regulation, for which he would be punished. When that failed, the interrogator would leave the room and a guard would apply the prescribed torture. The torture would not be halted until the prisoner gave in.

Sometimes it was possible to get away with providing a statement which would be transparently false or ridiculous to the Western world when released but would get past our captors. An example of this is the twenty-two-page statement of "biography" that I once wrote. Among other things it referred to the modest home in which I had been born and raised—a three-acre lot embracing a four-bedroom home complete with automatic washing machine, clothes dryer, soft couches and other nice furnishings, and many other desirable features which I listed in detail. I concluded this part of the statement with the words: "We were poor, of course. If we had been rich we would have been able to afford the luxuries."

If we occasionally got away with something like this, it was a costly joke when it was detected. Because our captors had only a poor understanding of English, absolutely no feel for its idiom, and no background of American ways and customs, they rarely saw through the prisoner's attempt to fool them. But if the written or typed account was one they decided to release to the world and as a result they learned of the deception, the prisoner concerned would be very harshly punished. Some POWs walked a very thin line in this respect, the North Vietnamese being suspicious but not quite sure. Usually of course the camp authorities would "get even" with such a man, using some other ostensible reason to punish him.

The prisoners had been subjected to rough treatment generally ever since the first one was captured, but as I understand it the tortures proper began in about October 1965, with Col. Robinson Risner as the first victim. It was then that the North Vietnamese started using various types of torture and maltreatment to extract propaganda statements from prisoners. My own initiation into a torture session came in October 1966. In this session they used two methods of torture. One was the tight handcuffs.

Regular handcuffs were a fact of POW life. We wore them whenever we moved between prisons, for example. They were usually worn during leg-iron punishment and always worn when in the "hole." Being metal they chafed the lower arms, but they were inconvenient rather than painful.

The tight cuffs used during torture sessions were quite another matter. Clamped around the lower part of each arm, they pushed the bones together and cut off the blood circulation, causing the wearer great pain. Some of the cuffs used incorporated a thumbscrew for tightening them still further.

Even wearing these barbaric devices was not necessarily the extent of one's problem. There were always the guards to reckon with. While blindfolded and wearing the tight cuffs during one torture session, my roommate Jim Ray was pushed into a rock-strewn hole five feet deep. (Miraculously he suffered no serious injury from the fall.) The guard then stomped on the cuffs on his arms and left. After some time, perspiration allowed Jim with great effort to move the cuffs slightly down the arm, but whenever he did this the guard would come in, move the cuffs up the arm again, and stomp on them.

In the torture session of October 1966 I got the second method rather than the tight cuffs. With my hands tied behind me I was made to run barefoot and blindfolded through a rocky and hilly area. The idea here was to make a man run into anything that was in the way, so that he would fall down and just hurt himself in general as well as hurting his feet in particular. Two guards took me, one on each arm, and made me run, letting go of me when I got to a tree or a wall or a hole, then hauling me up on my feet and forcing me to run again. When they got tired, fresh guards took their places. I found out that they could keep this up longer than I could and I finally succumbed to their wishes and wrote a statement condemning the war policy of the U.S. government. We understood that they were using these statements to support the North Vietnamese position at the Bertrand Russell Tribunal in Stockholm. After they broke me I felt very remorseful about it, as did every other prisoner in such circumstances.

My legs and arms and body were cut and bruised from falling down and running into things. As to my feet, they

were so badly bruised and cut up that I could barely walk
for the next three weeks or more. It was some time after
that before I could walk normally, the problems in my feet
then more or less phasing into the prolonged attack of beriberi which I have described in chapter 3.

Besides those methods already described, the North Vietnamese genius for cruelty found expression in several other
methods of torture, including one known as "the stool." I
have personally experienced that one. Here a man is seated
on a stool and left there, food being brought to him at the
regular times. (Food was not usually withheld during torture.)
Time and the guards do the rest. In process of time the man
gets sleepy, but whenever he falls asleep a guard comes in
and wakes him up by hitting him under the nose. Not on top
of the nose, because that might crack a bone. Under the nose
is a more tender spot and a blow there will not leave a
permanent mark. A refinement of this torture was to shackle
a man's ankles to the stool so that he was completely immobile.
As was fairly standard with prison punishments and tortures
the man could not even get up to relieve himself. One man
survived this treatment for twenty days before he broke. Most
of us couldn't take it that long.

Even when you finally gave way, that might not be the
end. In the last part of July and first part of August 1967 a
torture session was in process. This time it was the kneeling
and standing methods—very painful to the feet and legs. I
took this for about three days and nights before I broke and
gave my tormentors the statement they were asking for. Then
they wanted more—and I was subjected to more of the same
treatment to get it out of me.

Some of the tortures were more a matter of general
physical endurance than of suffering great pain, and the
length of each man's torture session would vary because of this
and other factors. Each man realized that the longer he could
hold out, the longer it would be before someone else had to
come in and endure the same thing, and since no one knew
when the session would cease there was always the hope that

by enduring longer one would save someone down the line. When the North Vietnamese wanted quick compliance with their demands however they knew how to get it. It seemed as if sometimes the orders would come down to them from higher authority for a rush job of production—producing propaganda statements by prisoners of war. At any rate, the really swift method was the ropes. No one could endure them for very long.

When I was given this treatment they tied my hands tightly behind my back, then put a rope around the upper arms and cinched the rope together, causing the extreme strain and pressure on the sternum which I have described previously. That was just the beginning. They now passed a rope from the rope around my arms up over the back of the neck and head and down to the front of my body, cinching it on the rope which tied my legs together near the ankles. The agony produced as they cinched the rope tighter and tighter is indescribable. A man might steel his will to endure perhaps an hour in this extreme position, but unless he passed out this would seem to me to be about the limit of human endurance. I know of no one who failed to be broken by this torture.

The Vietnamese of course wanted to maintain the myth of humane treatment, which is their reason for preferring torture methods which left no permanent mark. This may be the reason they did not use this rope method every time, perhaps only when they had a "rush job" on. Although they first wrapped the arms and legs with cloth to minimize scarring by ropes, it is obvious that such extreme brutality administered by careless or callous guards could in fact scar or maim somebody. It could even kill—people have had heart attacks under far less severe provocation. There is no doubt that some prisoners did in fact die under torture.

The irony of this in a way is that any one of the prisoners would have been willing to die for his country had that been required of him. Under the pain and despair of torture many a prisoner voiced this not merely with his mind and heart but with his lips, crying out to die and envying his comrades

who had done so in battle. Unfortunately that was not the
choice. The choice lay between continuing to endure an interminable pain with an increasingly ineffective will, and signing a statement which, under those conditions, it was not
difficult to convince oneself would be discredited by the free
world when published.

After continuous torture the will finally eroded to the
point where it no longer functioned. I wrote what my tormentors told me to write, I said what they wanted me to say.
If they said the North were winning in South Vietnam, I
agreed with them. If they said I was a criminal, I said I was a
criminal. Just about all of the prisoners in North Vietnamese
hands up to 1969 were severely tortured, and virtually all of
those tortured finally gave way.

While the torture session was in progress almost no
prisoner was free from its effects. If he had not yet been involved this time, there was a good chance that he would be;
at any time he might hear the jingling of keys in the hallway.
Whether or not he had had his turn this time he could never
be indifferent to the plight of those who had. One of the
worst experiences in prison was to hear a man somewhere in
the distance crying out "Help me! Help me!" and knowing
that there was nothing you could do except pray and ask
God to help that man. It was indeed an empty and terrible
feeling to be helpless at that moment, unable to assist someone
so desperately in need of help. We knew prison authorities
and guards to be sadistic and cruel. They broke bones in
torture, not always deliberately necessarily but because of
their careless and barbaric way of doing things. They pulled
ribs away from the sternum, they broke people's arms, they
broke people's ribs by beatings. So when you heard a cry
for help, you knew it was not makebelieve.

Sometimes of course the Vietnamese were asking for impossible confessions and information. One North Vietnamese
officer we referred to as Rabbit, having read in the *New York
Times* that Buzz Sawyer was flying EA6-B aircraft, had one
of the prisoners tortured to make him admit to flying an

EA6-B. If he had admitted this, the next questions would have sought information about this aircraft. Under the torture of the ropes on his arms the prisoner insisted, "I wasn't flying an EA6-B, I was flying an A-6." Rabbit wouldn't believe him and left the ropes on him.

As a result the victim lost the use of his hands. For three months he couldn't feed himself. For six months he couldn't clean himself. It took nine months before he had enough feeling back in his hands to shave himself.

Lack of medical care imposed its own tortures, some of them long sustained. One man got an infection in his bone just above the ankle and it ate away a couple of inches of bone. He walked on crutches for almost eight years in prison. Another prisoner sustained a dislocated shoulder when he landed after ejection from his aircraft. By the time he had suffered with the infection and the delays and with the operations the Vietnamese finally gave him, he was in serious danger of losing his life. He fought back and regained some of his strength. Fortunately he had a strong constitution and the will to live. But when he was released his left arm and shoulder were still in poor shape.

The hero of all heroes for most POWs was a man who took a direct hit while in the cockpit. He had flack spread all over his body, both wrists broken, and his feet and legs badly wounded. Stripped to his underwear by looters and racked with pain and weakness, he lay for days alternating between life and death, unable to sustain permanent consciousness but unwilling to surrender to death. At one point he was actually lowered into a hole which had been dug for his grave, but he managed to rouse himself and yell out, and his captors pulled him out of the hole again.

They put him in the back of a truck, and as it bounced along over the bumpy roads he was beaten so badly that he had raw spots worn to the bone all over his back, shoulderblades, and pelvic area. The guards, thinking either that he was dead or that he was too far gone for them to worry about, kicked him out of the truck when it was going about twenty miles an hour and left him there. He came to in a ditch.

Now this man somehow dragged himself by his elbows out of the ditch and over to a building a couple of hundred yards away, which took him several hours. In captivity again, he had such a strong will to live that he just wouldn't die. In a few days he was thrown in a truck again and transported in this way to Hanoi, which he reached eighteen days after shootdown.

This man received completely inadequate medical attention. His life was saved by the Lord's blessing, his own will-power, and the POW in whose cell he was put at Hanoi Hilton. That prisoner washed him, fed him, and did everything for him until he could help himself. Finally the North Vietnamese took him to a hospital, where their doctors worked on him and took care of some of his wounds. They cut about two inches of bone out of his right lower arm, then sewed the flesh and skin back again, leaving the arm a terrible-looking mess and the hand immobile. For $4\frac{1}{2}$ years one leg had an open sore about 10 inches long, $\frac{1}{4}$ inch wide and $\frac{1}{4}$ inch deep that was running with pus and infection. It was still like that when he was released.

For all their neglect and cruelty the North Vietnamese did not break our spirit. Admittedly they could break us temporarily and make us do things we would not normally have done, but though we were regretful of having done them we recognized them as an inevitable thing in the circumstances and we were not permanently broken in spirit by the experience. We always bounced back to fight again. Because of our unity, because we kept faith with each other, we could recover our spirit even though we knew that any time the North Vietnamese really wanted anything they could get it from us. It was our job to see that we gave them as much trouble as we could to get it, to minimize their gains. This we always tried to do.

When times were at their toughest there was a tendency for more spiritual reflection anyway, and I believe most of us pondered then upon the great suffering of Christ. Everything is relative. What we were enduring for our country was more than most have been asked to do, yet it was so little compared with what Christ endured for us. It was natural to think about that. I know that I did many times.

Even in prison, some POWs were required to endure a lot more than others. Some of our senior officers in particular earned our sincere respect in this matter, for generally speaking the more senior officers suffered more torture sessions than the rest of us, propaganda statements from them being put at a higher value. Apart of course from length of captivity, other factors must have had their effect. Compared with many POWs I did not have to endure a great deal of torture. This may have been partly because I was sick so much of the time, especially in the first four years or so when the torture was prevalent. Presumably it was not worthwhile for the North Vietnamese to torture me too often in those circumstances and thus perhaps incur the trouble and expense of having to give me medical treatment. They had no need to give themselves this problem. After all, there were always plenty of potential victims to choose from.

There have been many definitions of a communist. Our experience in prison gave us another: "A communist is a person who will torture you to write a statement that you have not been tortured."

Among other things, our captors did just that.

Chapter 6

TIME THE ESSENCE

In our prison camps I was never forced to do any hard labor as such. We did have a few work projects like sweeping the yard to keep it clean, sweeping up the leaves, pulling weeds, and so on, but I myself was never forced to work. There were many times when I would gladly have been outside working instead of being cooped up in a cell, but the opportunities were rare. The camp authorities did ask us prisoners to go out and help fill up craters made by U.S. bombs, working with the people to show them we had no hard feelings, but we all refused to do that. Compliance would have been interpreted as regret for the bombings, of which we had no such feelings; and by photograph as well as by radio and other media the North Vietnamese would have made much propaganda out of the incident.

Lack of outside activities accentuated a problem all POWs were concerned about in prison—how to get the exercise to keep in reasonable condition, especially while cooped up in small cells. Some kind of exercise program was a "must" for every man, and its implementation was a good way of using up time. It had a drawback, of course—it made us hungrier when already we did not have enough food. But this was a price we felt we had to pay.

Apart from his physical condition, a man's exercise program varied according to the size of his body, his cell, and his ambition. I'm rather small compared with most men there, and in addition I found that the more strenuous types of exercise were impracticable during the years of sickness and general debility. As a result I just about had to settle for walking. Accordingly I would pace back and forth in the cell. In the smaller rooms, this meant three paces one way then three the other way—ad infinitum, it seemed. It was during this exercise that I did a lot of my thinking.

Other men had more ambitious programs, frequently on a competitive basis. Situps, pushups, and deep knee-bends were possible in even the smallest cells (even if they had to be done on the wooden bed), and some of the larger men in particular reached fantastic levels of achievement in these.

As with our other self-help programs, the exercise efforts reached their peak in the competitive brotherhood of the forty-eight-man room we moved into in November 1970. Under mutually agreed rules some men reached the several-hundred level in pushups and situps, for example. There too for the first time it was practicable to run—only just, but it could be done. Forty-three laps around the two-foot wide surround to the "island" we slept on constituted a mile. Each morning, running barefoot, ten or twelve men lapped one or two miles around this special track.

How else did we occupy our time in prison? We talked with roommates (when we had any) about food, as I have mentioned, but even that subject had its interest limitations. At much cost in time and effort we covertly passed information between the different cells. We shared whatever knowledge we had brought with us. We shared our thoughts After all this, there was still much waking time left in the day. Inevitably, in the smaller cells especially, each man was left for long periods with his own thoughts.

For all of us, thoughts of home absorbed most of this thinking time. Thoughts of America, yes, but even more so of home and loved ones; old familiar surroundings; childhood and youth; and especially, wife and children.

Throughout the years of prison I reflected more upon my younger life than at any other period of time—the years I lived on the farm in Arco, Idaho, with my grandmother, and the enjoyable times I had with friends during my high school years. I was about five when we moved to Arco, Idaho, in Lost River Valley. My mother, my brother and I lived there while my father was working in Idaho Falls. It was a little two-room house with a coal stove to cook on and heat the house. There was no car or phone.

I started school in Arco, and three years later we moved back to Burley, Idaho, the city of my birth. There I went to school, returning each summer to Arco to spend three months on the farm with my grandmother and riding racehorses as a jockey for her neighbor, Harold Anderson. I had my own horse too—Tony. Those were great days.

I enjoyed living with Grandmother Chesley. I would lie on the prison bed recalling the tremendous influence she has had on my life. She taught me much, both by precept and example. She taught me about religion and life and encouraged me always to live right. I went to church with her in the summers, but home in Burley my parents did not go to church so I would slack off there.

When I was eleven some friends got me interested in becoming a Boy Scout and I started going to church. On December 25, 1949, my cousin Sherman Vaughn and I went in to Bishop Lawrence Tolman and asked him if we could be baptized that day. He smiled and asked, "What have your parents said about that?" We replied: "Well, our parents don't know, but they won't care whether we are baptized or not."

The bishop talked with us for a while, then said: "I have to walk by your house on my way home, and I'll stop by and ask your parents if it's okay." He did so, and our parents gave permission. In fact they drove us up to the baptism, but they didn't come in the building. Sherman and I walked home afterwards. I well remember that cold Christmas Day in 1949. The baptism was a big event in my life and I felt very happy about it.

I continued to go to church, graduated from Primary, and started in the Scouting program. Being an Eagle Scout had a lot of prestige. I worked hard to achieve that goal and had the satisfaction of becoming the first one in our troop to make it.

About that time, my dad became active in the Church again. Oddly enough, around that time too I started falling away from Church practices even though I continued to attend meetings. I started to smoke and drink a little beer. This continued from about the time I was fifteen or sixteen through high school. When the mother of the girl I was going with during my senior year made us break up, I joined the air force (on the rebound, so to speak) after graduation. Then in February 1957 I went back to Burley on leave and married another girl I had graduated with from high school.

We had only a month together, then I was sent to Japan for two years. I had been in Japan for just about a year when I received a letter from her asking me for a divorce. It crushed me. I didn't want a divorce. I told her I would do anything to save our marriage, but she was adamant. Finally I consented and she got a divorce.

That "Dear John" letter was probably the best thing that ever happened to me because it impelled me to change direction. I stopped drinking and smoking, tried to put my life in order, and began attending church. There were not many LDS in our group, and consequently each of us had the opportunity to hold varied Church positions. It was in Japan that I was ordained an elder.

I spent a few days at home in 1959, then I was assigned to Germany. Immediately on arrival I was again immersed in LDS group activities. I had many faith-promoting experiences in that land.

I got out of the air force in June of 1960 and moved back to Burley. I didn't look for a good job in case it should tempt me not to go to college. Instead I worked in a garage washing cars and cleaning up for $1.25 an hour. During that summer I met JoDene. That fall we were married.

I started school at Weber College in Ogden, Utah, in September of 1960. By May 1963 I had finished a four-year curriculum in less than three years, graduated with honors, worked full-time at Boeing Aircraft virtually the entire time I was in college, and my wife and I had one child, Debbie. I was quite proud of that accomplishment. I was proud of my wife too, because she never complained or griped even though we had almost nothing. We had enough to eat and that was about all. JoDene stood beside me and encouraged me in all ways. She was a good wife and a good mother.

Under the pressures of work, the college schedule, and financial hardship, we were on-and-off active in the Church. We tried to live the gospel in our personal lives.

JoDene stood by me too in my desire to be a pilot. She had our second child, Don, while I was at Officers Training School at the end of 1963. When I was having a hard time learning to fly at Webb AFB she encouraged me in every way and prayed with me that I would be able to get my wings, never complaining because I was away from her a lot.

In our longing to be with our families I suppose most of the prisoners tended to idealize our wives and children, reflecting only on their good points and planning for them the life we would like them to aspire to. I know I did this. I planned the good times we would have together, the things JoDene and I would learn together, how I would help the children with their schooling. I thought about how I wanted the children to be studious but not to be bookworms, to participate in plays, to be cheerleaders, to play musical instruments, to do all the things I never was good enough to do myself. I wanted them to have many opportunities that I had not had. Most of all I wanted them to go to church, gain a testimony of the gospel, and live its principles.

AUTHOR AT WEBB AFB DURING PILOT TRAINING

Reviewing the past and planning for the future were psychologically and spiritually important but we were in great need too of the stimulus of ideas and information. Years without a pencil and paper or a book can seem very long indeed. Our hunger for knowledge was almost as great as our hunger for food—in some respects, perhaps even greater. How different it might have been if I had had just one good book—preferably the scriptures, but even Shakespeare or a dictionary, for example! In prison we were so hungry for reading material that the labels on our occasional packages from home (before the authorities started taking them from us) were probably a greater joy to us even than eating the goodies. We spent hours studying those labels—reading the instructions, spelling out the ingredients, calculating the weights from listed details, and reveling in every way in the delights of this printed word.

My hunger for knowledge was stimulated by the deprivation, of course. It was not always there previously. As with most young people, I suppose, I had gone to college not with a yearning for true education but with the goal of getting out of college as fast as I could, of getting the grades and the diploma. I achieved that goal without learning much, then promptly forgot what I *had* learned. I have a different outlook on education now. I am going back to college for more education, and this time what I really care about is knowledge. With that I will be able to get the grades. Previously I got the grades without the knowledge.

This reaction was a common one in the prison. Grades and diplomas had served all of us well in the world of America. But in the world bounded by the prison walls they were not of much value. The question rather was how much a man knew.

When each of us lived alone or in small groups, we tried to help each other learn through our communication system. It was quite difficult to do so by this remote-control method, especially without books or writing materials, but I did learn a couple of thousand words in Spanish from a young man in another room who had studied the language in high school and college. He would give me ten words a day and I would put them in my memory bank. Each day I would go through every word again; then I would get from him ten more and add them to my mental list. I would review the entire list two or three times each day to keep the words familiar in my mind. No doubt the absence of instructional materials made for some inaccuracies but the demanding mental approach probably induced a greater concentration and consequently more effective learning.

In those days too we used the memory bank for another very important purpose: we each made it a point to commit to memory the name of each POW and some brief biographical detail about him. We never knew what the future held, what circumstances might some day give some of us our freedom, and any one of us could have told who was in captivity and carried to a man's loved ones some news about him. As time went on, of course, this became less important because virtually everyone was intermittently receiving and sending mail. Nevertheless some fellows kept this mental list going until the last stages of our captivity.

When we were put in the big room in November 1970 it made a tremendous difference. Now we had far greater opportunities to pass the time profitably. Among other things we set up an educational program which would tap the knowledge resources of the forty-eight men in the room.

We broke a piece of brick from the wall and, writing on the concrete floor, listed a number of subjects—American history, psychology, sociology, physiology, religion, French, Spanish, German, trigonometry, and so on. Against each subject we wrote the name of the man who would teach it. I elected to teach religion. Interestingly the highest level of interest was shown in American history and the next level in religion. The men wanted to know most about their country and their God.

In my religion course I taught my roommates the Bible as best I knew it. I taught them the names of the books, the

different categories of books, their significance, and what detail
I could remember from various books. It took me about a
year, teaching mainly on Sundays, but I finally exhausted my
knowledge of the Bible. I did not try to push my religion in
such larger groups, though I did teach privately anyone who
was interested. Most of the men showed that interest.

After I had taught this class for a year, with the aid
here and there of some of the other men in the room, we
started group discussions on related topics. One of these was
the home storage of food for use in emergencies. I explained
the policy and procedures of the Church on this matter and
we discussed the subject in "round-table" discussions on several occasions. In similar discussions we also took up the subject of being better husbands and fathers. The topic of family
home evening was discussed in this connection, and I explained
the Church program on this. Some of the men concluded
that after being released they would inaugurate a family
home evening program in their families.

A big attraction was the language courses. We were
fortunate to have in our room two who knew French, two
Spanish, and one German. Here was an answer to my long-
expressed prayer for a roommate who would teach me a
foreign language. I studied French and Spanish and got along
fairly well in both.

We even had music lessons. Again using a piece of brick,
the teacher drew on the floor an enlarged illustration of a
section of a piano keyboard. He identified the pitch of each
"key" and allocated one key to each student. Having taught
each man his note, he directed the students as they played
simple tunes by hopping on and off the keys. Similarly he
taught us chords by having three or four stand on their respective keys simultaneously. This novel method of instruction
was not only extremely interesting but very amusing.

In the group was a fellow who in earlier years had been
an instructor in the Arthur Murray dance studio program.
Our floor space was a little cramped for dancing, but we made
a brave effort as under his direction we alternated between the

male and female dancing roles. Like the music lessons, the dancing lessons were great fun as well as being instructive.

While our education program naturally leaned heavily on lecture classes on formal subjects, it embraced also evening programs varying widely in content and format. Acting on the principle that an idle mind is the devil's workshop, each evening we would have a program of some kind to fill the otherwise empty space and make time pass more quickly. In this way each man got a chance to discuss his hobby or special interest. As an example, in the room we had an expert on skeet shooting and he told us all the positions and rules for skeet. Another night we might have a talk on Grand Prix racing, the speaker telling us about the cars, the drivers, the course, and so on. On another occasion we might have a presentation on Yellowstone Park, or horse racing, or some other subject one of the men knew well. Frequently these presentations were entertaining as well as educational.

On Saturdays and Sundays we would have movie reviews or book reports—sometimes both or a combination of the two. These always made an interesting program, partly because many present would have seen the movie or read the book. At the end of the year we would have academy awards for the best movie, the best scenes, etc. We had a lot of fun at this.

Even more interesting and enjoyable was a program we called the Cabbage Bowl. It was faintly reminiscent of the G.E. College Bowl, except that this was for cabbage heads— that was us!

We had four sections in our room with twelve guys in each and three teams of three participating in each section. In the Cabbage Bowl each section would compete against every other section. The guys that were not on the panel that night made up the questions. A question was asked and the first panelist to hold up his hand would answer. Since we had no printed material to check the answers with, in case of disagreement (and there naturally was some disagreement) the majority ruled. I was pretty happy because our section was undefeated. We won three in a row to be the room winners. We all had a lot of fun doing this, but it was enlightening as well because it gave a man a feel of how his general knowledge compared with that of others.

Religion was one of the categories used for the questions. I noted with pleasure that those who had been in my Sunday classes did well in these programs.

Another interesting thing we did was to hold presidential elections in 1968 and 1972. In the first one this was held simply among the twenty men in our seven-room cell block. In 1972 the voting took place among the 208 men in thirteen buildings of the northern camp near the Chinese border. While this disclosure may not throw the Gallup poll out of whack, the vote both times was overwhelmingly in favor of Richard Nixon.

On all special occasions and U.S. holidays—the Fourth of July, Christmas Day, Easter, and so on—we would have appropriate programs. Some of these special programs were outstanding. The theme to almost all of them was patriotism, our love for our country. We took opportunity constantly to remind ourselves of the privilege we enjoyed in being citizens of the United States of America.

One Fourth of July, one of the men living in another room went out to the bath area dressed in blue long johns, red shorts, and a white towel. I don't know where he got the odd clothes from—perhaps in a package from home, since some were receiving packages occasionally by this time. In our room we hung red, white and blue towels, or anything else we had that was red, white and blue, on a line in a prominent place. At this time we hadn't made a flag. Later we did.

I guess one of the most significant things that helped us hang on over there was a sense of humor, being able to laugh at each other and ourselves. Towards the end, when we had a little less restriction on our movements, we used to watch one prisoner ride his "motorcycle" around the camp. He would polish it and wash it—he even had a helmet made out of something or other. He had the high handlebars, and he would kick-start the bike and make all the appropriate noises as he rode it around. Of course all of this was imaginary, but he really entertained the other prisoners. The Vietnamese authorities didn't know what to make of him. He had them all flustered. They probably thought he was crazy. One day the camp commander told him he was not allowed to ride his motorcycle any more because there wasn't room in the yard; and besides, the other prisoners didn't have motorcycles.

We had some riotous times laughing at some of the silly little things that happened. I think I may have laughed harder in prison than I have ever laughed at anything in my life. We put on some skits and some commercials that were really hilarious. Often we would be poking fun at another roommate, but we all got our turn and everyone seemed to take it in good spirit. We put on musicals such as "South Pacific" and "The Sound of Music," with costumes, "girlies," and everything. It was a very entertaining program.

I remember Christmas Day 1970. We were putting on a skit when the camp commander and five or six other high-ranking Vietnamese officials crawled up on top of a water trough to look in our window and watch. They didn't say anything. Most likely they couldn't believe their eyes.

Perhaps my most impressive recollection of the things I occupied my time with was my learning about twenty poems. As with the classical music I heard on those two Sundays in the early days, the poetry did something for my soul. The poems may not have been word-for-word accurate the way I learned them, coming as they did from other people's memories, but that made no difference to the compelling messages. Two in particular that encouraged and strengthened me were William E. Henley's "Invictus," which I believe is Latin for *unconquered,* and Rudyard Kipling's "If."

To fit my convictions I changed the third line of "Invictus" to read "I thank the God I know to be." I am conscious too that there is a certain lack of humility in the poet's ex-

pressions and that I personally would wish to give the Lord
full credit for his assistance in the dark days behind me. But
Henley's poem does at least typify a spirit unconquered by
circumstances, a spirit we tried to emulate in prison.

> Out of the night that covers me,
> Black as the pit from pole to pole,
> I thank whatever gods may be
> For my unconquerable soul.
>
> In the fell clutch of circumstance
> I have not winced nor cried aloud.
> Under the bludgeonings of chance
> My head is bloody, but unbow'd.
>
> Beyond this place of wrath and tears
> Looms but the Horror of the shade,
> And yet the menace of the years
> Finds and shall find me unafraid.
>
> It matters not how strait the gate,
> How charged with punishments the scroll,
> I am the master of my fate:
> I am the captain of my soul.

Kipling's poem too contained thoughts which lifted my
heart and helped to give me strength during the dark days.
"Hold on!" it said.

> If you can keep your head when all about you
>   Are losing theirs and blaming it on you,
> If you can trust yourself when all men doubt you,
>   But make allowance for their doubting too;
> If you can wait and not be tired by waiting,
>   Or being lied about, don't deal in lies,
> Or being hated, don't give way to hating,
>   And yet don't look too good, nor talk too wise;
>
> If you can dream—and not make dreams your master;
>   If you can think—and not make thoughts your aim;

If you can meet with Triumph and Disaster
    And treat those two impostors just the same;
If you can bear to hear the truth you've spoken
    Twisted by knaves to make a trap for fools,
Or watch the things you gave your life to, broken,
    And stoop and build 'em up with worn-out tools:

If you can make one heap of all your winnings
    And risk it on one turn of pitch-and-toss,
And lose, and start again at your beginnings
    And never breathe a word about your loss;
If you can force your heart and nerve and sinew
    To serve your turn long after they are gone,
And so hold on when there is nothing in you
    Except the Will which says to them: "Hold on!"

If you can talk with crowds and keep your virtue,
    Or walk with kings—nor lose the common touch,
If neither foes nor loving friends can hurt you,
    If all men count with you, but none too much;
If you can fill the unforgiving minute
    With sixty seconds' worth of distance run,
Yours is the Earth and everything that's in it,
    And—which is more—you'll be a Man, my son!

As well as these two poems the Twenty-Third Psalm was
a source of great inspiration to us. We repeated it and talked
about it often, especially in our church services. Even more
than its outstanding literary value we felt its spiritual power,
the power to make us ever conscious that God had not for-
gotten us.

The nearly seven years I spent as a prisoner of war would
have been long enough to get a Ph.D. in America. None of
us came out with that distinction. But from our experiences
I believe we have learned many things a university can't
teach. I like to hope those experiences have somehow improved my character.

Chapter 7

NO ATHEISTS IN HELL HOLES

During World War II someone coined the phrase, "There are no atheists in foxholes." My observation was that this was true too among the U.S. prisoners of war in the hell hole of Hoa Lo or other prison camps in North Vietnam. It seems that hardship and danger sharpen the religious instincts— or rather, make people feel toward God.

Since my return many people have asked me what I think about our prisoners of war finding God in prison. As perhaps in the "foxhole" statement, the implication is that such a "finding" might be temporary only. I think that most men I knew in prison were sincerely religious. Most of them prayed to God asking for strength and guidance. Nevertheless as things got easier after 1969 I thought I could see my friends around me slacking up somewhat in religious expression. What are the chances of the men continuing religious observances now they are home? I am asked. I believe the answer is that those who took God to prison will have brought God home with them, while with a few exceptions those who did not will have left him there.

I was fortunate to have found God earlier. I did wrong things in my early life, things I am very sorry about and of which I have repented. I have found the Lord to be very willing to forgive.

My family have all profited by this willingness on the Lord's part. My parents were inactive in the Church for

—*Church News photo, J. M. Heslop, photographer*

VERL R. AND SUSIE CHESLEY WITH SON LARRY

many years. They would send my brother and me to church each Sunday with a neighbor, Harold Anderson and his family. Because they admired the Andersons' way of life, one day my parents went to church with them. But this time it didn't take. After four or five Sundays, Dad found an excuse not to go back.

After about twenty years of inactivity, Dad got lured back into the Church in early 1951 by a David Tracy, a man who wouldn't give up. He somehow got Dad to go ward teaching, then to priesthood meeting. In May of 1952 the stake president spoke to Dad, apparently casually, on how he would feel about a leadership position. He almost panicked at the thought, having done nothing in the Church yet but ward teaching. But he was ordained an elder on June 8 that year, went through the temple on July 8, and was installed as bishop of a newly created ward on July 13. He learned a lot in his eight years as bishop, but nothing more important than the Lord's willingness to forgive us.

I had joined the Church two or three years before Dad's return, but true conversion came years later following some wayward years I'd rather forget. My actions must have distressed my parents in their new life. I must also have displeased my Heavenly Father. During those years I wasn't paying much attention to either earthly or heavenly parents.

In particular, I've had a lot of heartache over my failure to follow a specific piece of counsel. It came in my patriarchal blessing given by Alfred Knight, the stake patriarch when I was sixteen. It told me in specific terms to settle for no other kind of marriage but a temple marriage. It gave good reasons and was emphatic on the point.

Despite this I impulsively married young in a civil marriage. Within eighteen months I bitterly regretted this step. The ensuing emotional stress awakened within me my need for God. I found him, together with the needed Church activity and companionship, in Japan and Germany during my first air force hitch.

It was here that I got my first real experience in the spiritual side of life. It was here I came to realize that people are the important part of true religion—our Father's other children. People have been important to me ever since, and I have greatly enjoyed meeting and associating with new acquaintances and friends. That's one reason I have enjoyed the air force. This response to others, and a genuine desire to see the best in people, was also a great help during my years as a prisoner of war.

In terms of people, my religious life was sparked by Don Hathaway, an air force master sergeant and a convert to the Church, who treated me like a son. In Japan he consoled and encouraged me during very dark days. There and later in Germany he was always concerned. After about the third time he had towed me back to base in Germany when my '49 Chev had broken down, once 140 miles away, he said to me: "Larry, it's pretty nice to know that someone loves you, isn't it? Someone you can call on in time of need." In such impressive ways he reminded me of God's love for me.

I had many spiritual, faith-promoting experiences in Germany. There was the moving riverside baptism service in Bavaria on a cold April day and the radiant young convert I met there; the vibrant testimony and conversion story of Edna Bush, and her ardent desire that her husband should join the Church;[1] the magnificently spiritual conference at Berchtesgaden, Adolph Hitler's one-time retreat; and particularly the experience Dick Messenger and I had in blessing a baby.

Dick, whom I first met in Germany, is my good friend. We were working on my old car when the phone call came. Would we go to the army hospital and administer to a baby there? We cleaned up, then knelt in prayer together. I prayed hard to know the Lord's will in the matter.

Dick was a corpsman in the hospital, and he quickly found the anxious parents. The mother was a Church mem-

---

[1]Edna Bush tells her conversion story in the book *No More Strangers*, by Hartman & Connie Rector, published by Bookcraft in 1971. Her husband Lester Bush joined the Church in 1973.

ber, the father was not. I said to the father: "We are elders
in The Church of Jesus Christ of Latter-day Saints. Your
wife has called us to administer to your baby by the priesthood
authority we hold. Do you think we can do any good if we
do so?" He replied, "Yes, I do. Will you please bless our
baby."

With the doctor's approval we removed the oxygen tent
while Dick anointed the baby's head with oil and I pronounced
a blessing on him. I was impelled to say that the baby would
become whole and go home. I felt full of faith and power
from God as I prayed and blessed that baby. It was a tremendous spiritual moment.

That night when Dick went to work the baby was gone.
When Dick inquired, the doctor told him that the baby had
been bleeding internally and losing strength but in the previous
few hours had recovered and now had gone home; that whatever was wrong had somehow righted itself.

How wonderful that God had answered my prayers in
this way! I thought about such experiences a great deal in
prison. They were another link with God. He had answered
my prayers then and would do so now.

It's strange how we can be active in the Church, as I
was in Germany and later, yet still miss significant points in
actually living the gospel. When I got out of the air force the
first time I ought to have remembered that patriarchal blessing. My mother had sent it to me in Japan, underlining the
part about marrying in the temple and emphasizing that the
unhappiness of my first marriage stemmed from my failure
to comply with it. Yet still when I remarried in 1960 I again
settled for a civil marriage. I am a slow learner, it seems.
Or perhaps this was a recurrence of the old confusions which
had plagued my teen-age years.

I did my best to correct the mistake in December 1961
when my marriage was sealed in the temple. By this time
we had our baby daughter Debbie. It was a moist-eyed occasion, with Debbie gazing around her in bright-eyed wonder

and bringing the feeling almost of an angelic presence from the other world she had recently left. This was another memorable spiritual experience I frequently called from the recesses of memory while in prison.

I had many fine gospel discussions with POWs not of my faith during my captivity, and many of these men evinced a great deal of interest in the gospel and the Church as I explained them. I cannot say that I was responsible there for a single conversion, though I did my best by word and example. They all knew what I was and what I stood for, and though they did not share my beliefs I know they respected me for them. It is my hope that my association with them there will in some way make the gospel message acceptable to some of them when they hear it again later in life.

Stimulating as the discussions often were with men of other faiths, the real joy of soul-sharing came in time spent with another who shared my convictions. I didn't meet all the LDS men in captivity. Of those I did meet, some were not very active in the Church though fine men personally. Two with strong testimonies whose paths crossed mine were Majors Jay Hess and Jay Jensen.

I never lived in the same room with Jay Hess, though I knew of him by repute since he and I were in the same building. He has a tremendous testimony of the gospel; and he had the reputation of being unflappable, of never getting angry. He was obviously an excellent representative of the Church.

Jay Jensen and I lived in the same large room with others for about a year. I found that Jay had strong convictions about the gospel and had served in some leadership positions in the Church. I learned a lot from Jay.

Jay and I were good for each other. We cheered each other up, gave each other comfort, I believe. We talked about each other's problems, and we told each other the things we had done wrong in the past and how we planned on living better in the future. We tried to strengthen each other, to encourage each other to do the things we knew we should do. I think it helped.

It was especially good to be able to discuss the principles of the gospel with someone who believed in them. Together too we recalled some of the LDS hymns we had sung since childhood. Using our improvised ink made from water and dirt we would write on toilet paper the words of the hymns we could remember. Sometimes we would sing them—just to ourselves, since neither of us could sing very well. Sometimes we would repeat the words as we thought together about the messages in our LDS songs.

I had a great affection for every man in that large room, but between Jay and me there was an extra bond of friendship. We were of the same faith, had the same concepts of God, had the same basic beliefs. We just related with each other. His sorrows were my own, his joys mine too, and vice versa. It was a testimony to me of what the gospel could do for the world in terms of love and friendship.

I was tremendously grateful in prison for my Church experience, and particularly when it came to conducting church services in prison. As I have explained previously, we had a small "service" on Sundays even when we were each in small cells, but after November 1970, when forty-eight of us were in the large room, we were able to do much better in this matter.

The prison authorities did not really like us holding church service. They did not like us to sing. Nevertheless as the situation eased we did hold church services and we even had a small choir. The choir would practice about three times a week for thirty or forty minutes a time. On the first few Sundays some of the prison officers came in and listened to the service. Apparently they were afraid we would create trouble and disorder by singing rousing songs and giving vigorous talks. When they saw that we were observing our ritual as Christians they accepted that, and they only bothered us on a few occasions after that.

We did not have a chaplain as such. My assignment in the area of religion, which I referred to in chapter 6, was educational rather than spiritual. Virtually all the men except myself were accustomed to church services conducted by a full-time minister, so they were not well prepared to give sermons. Most of them had never expressed themselves publicly on religion. Nevertheless the opportunity was given to every man in the room, if he desired to do so, to conduct our weekly religious service.

To me the results were surprising. I was immensely impressed by the spiritual uplift I received from those meetings. I suppose our circumstances had a lot to do with the effect, but as I look back I feel that some of my choicest spiritual experiences came out of those meetings in that dingy room. The man conducting could do what he wished. He could do the whole thing himself or ask others to participate. Usually we would first sing a couple of hymns, then have a prayer, then maybe a scripture, another hymn, then a sermon. There would then be a closing hymn and a closing prayer. After that we would pledge our allegiance to the flag and then sing a patriotic song.

The hymns we sang were frequently the well-known ones, the hymns Christians have sung for a century or two. They were always uplifting. I was particularly impressed by a verse one of the prisoners wrote to the tune of Billy Graham's theme song, "How Great Thou Art." He designed it for our circumstances, and we sang it with great feeling.

> In foreign lands you're even there to guide me.
> Your Holy Spirit in my heart yet dwells.
> When nights are cold, I feel your light inside me
> Imparting warmth to these cold, hostile cells.

Stories from a couple of the sermons stand out in my mind. A man named Jay told us a moving one. He had been stationed in England when orders came to go to Vietnam. Everything was rushed. Bound for San Antonio, Texas, where

the family was going to live in his absence, they stopped
off in South Carolina to visit some family members. After a
hectic three or four days in the area, Jay was visiting his
brother on his last night in South Carolina. Wanting to talk
to his brother, he and his wife had put their children to bed
a little early.

The children had been in bed about twenty minutes when
the older boy called out. Generally when they needed something the children would call their mother, but tonight the
boy was calling "Dad! Dad!" Jay was just a little peeved
when he went to the boy's bed, thinking he perhaps needed
a drink of water, or that the excitement had brought on a
stomachache. So as he approached the bed his voice was a
little gruff as he asked, "Yes, David, what it it?"

David looked up at his father and said, "Dad, I love
you."

"I love you too, son," Jay responded.

"I just wanted to tell you that, Dad," said David.

As Jay walked downstairs he was unhappy with himself
for being irritated at his son on the way up. He knew that
David had waited twenty minutes to be sure his younger
brother would be asleep because it didn't seem manly to David
to say "I love you," and he didn't want his little brother to
hear him say it.

There were many moist eyes in the group as big, six-foot-
two Jay related that story. Home was close to our hearts at
that moment. We all missed our children and hated being
absent from them during those vital years of their develop-
ment which would never return.

Another sermon gave an analogy concerning a fine land
to whose people one day a man came and gave everyone a
large hot-air balloon. With the balloon each person could
now travel to a certain land which was much more beautiful
than their own. The man gave instructions on how to use the

balloon and some of the people took off. But they got into difficulties: air turbulence blew the balloons around; little rocks tossed by the wind made holes in them, some air escaped, and they didn't rise fast enough; and they turned out to be difficult to steer and navigate.

The man who had brought the balloons had said: "Not only have I given you a balloon, but if you ask for them I will give you patches for it. It takes a little work but you can patch your balloons and then you will be able to go higher. Also I will give you navigational aids and instructions by radio along the way, if you will go from one checkpoint to another." Nevertheless many of the balloons drifted off course, ending up in the rocks and in deserts and not at the beautiful land which had been their original destination.

This seemed to me to be a beautiful analogy of Christ coming and giving us the gospel; giving us the gift of repentance to patch our balloons with; offering us help if we will ask for it; giving us signboards along the way to help us reach our destination. All this to help us get back into that beautiful place, heaven.

One of the men told a story both sad and humorous. When his father was on the council of one of the Protestant churches, he told us, they were in need of money and the question of personal contributions was discussed. One of the rich guys on the council made the statement, "Those people who don't pay money for its support aren't welcome in this church." At this the storyteller's father had looked at the rich man with something approaching contempt and said, "Let me tell you a story."

He told of a family that moved near to a rich area in Dallas, Texas. They were good people but relatively poor, cleanly but not well dressed. They began going to a church attended mainly by rich people, and the members of the congregation were hostile toward them. Later the members told the minister he would have to tell the new family that they were not welcome in that church.

The minister pleaded that everyone was welcome in his church, but to no avail. He got the word, "If you want to keep your job here, go and tell them."

Finally the minister acquiesced. "I'm sorry, you're not welcome in our church," he told the father of the poorer family. "It's not my doing, but you can't come any more." Of course the man pleaded with him. "We have been of this faith all of our lives," he protested, "and yours is the church closest to us." But he had to give in. He stopped taking his family to that church.

Several weeks later the minister's conscience got the better of him and he went back to the man. "I'm sorry about what I told you," he said. "You are welcome in our church. Come back!"

The man looked at him for a moment before responding. "No, that's okay," he said, "I shouldn't really expect to get into that church. I had a long talk with the Lord, and the Lord told me that he had been trying to get into that church for about twenty years and still hadn't made it."

For our weekly services we hung homemade American flags and a cross. To make the cross we first made a crude needle then tore thread from a blanket and sewed cut-up pieces of a handerchief to a red towel in the form of a cross. This cross has since been sent to the air force museum at Wright-Patterson AFB.

Our weekly services of course were held without the benefit of any literature to assist us. Like other literature, the Bible was denied us for general use and we had to do the best we could by putting passages together from memory. As a special concession, however, we would be allowed to have a copy of the Bible on Christmas Day for an hour to copy the Christmas story and for an hour at Easter to copy the Easter story, so that our services on those two occasions would be a little more enlightening. This happened after we got into the large room in November 1970. Before that we did not have use of the Bible even to that limited extent.

Church services and Bible reading are in any case only a part of religion, one's conduct and attitudes being a more significant part. Concern for each other played a strong part in our prison life, as I have indicated in another chapter, and there were many instances of Christian service right there among the prisoners. No doubt too we all reflected a great deal on our behavior during the easier life of the past.

There was comfort to me in knowing that I had at least been on the right track before my capture and making sincere efforts to live by Christian standards. In earlier days my father had said to me: "Larry, follow the path of a leader, because you have some leadership qualities that are needed in this country. And remember to lead in the right paths." I recall my mother saying: "Larry, when you're away from home in the military, sometimes it may not be easy to kneel down beside your bed without being ridiculed. But always have a prayer in your heart. You can always do that. With that the Lord will look after you."

As I left home in 1965 to go to Vietnam, my father, who is not an emotional man, threw his arms around me and said simply, "Be a good boy, son." And I replied, "I will, Dad, I promise you I will." I made some minor mistakes, but I kept that promise to the best of my ability.

I suppose the unspoken emphasis in my father's charge to me was the moral one, the matter of chastity. Being a pilot and away from my wife from time to time on flying duties, I had lacked neither opportunity nor temptation to break this high-priority commandment of God. In prison I thought a great deal about the importance of this commandment. How glad I was then that I had kept myself morally clean, and that in my years of marriage to JoDene I had never even kissed another girl, other than perhaps relatives! I am sure I could have been a better husband, but at least I had been true. The prison years had their own way of shutting out any temptations of female companionship. As to the revolting sin of homosexuality, so far as I know it simply did not exist among the prisoners. I never heard of a single instance of it.

I discussed the principle of chastity with various other POWs, often in the context of a gospel discussion. One of them had been unfaithful to his wife on many occasions. He felt that he was a good husband—a gentleman to his wife, always opened the car door for her, and so on. But when he was away from his wife he would run around with other women and commit adultery. Interestingly, one of his comments was that it would break his heart if his wife were untrue to him. I asked him what the difference was, why the double standard. He didn't have an answer.

I had talked to this man a lot about the Church and he seemed quite interested in our doctrines. As we discussed this particular principle, he felt regret and remorse in retrospect, and he made a promise to himself and to me that he would never be unfaithful to his wife again. I believe he will honor that pledge and that if he truly repents the Lord will forgive him for his wrongdoing.

In prison I needed all the good health I could get and that means I observed the Word of Wisdom. There were occasions now and then when the only liquid available was tea, and then I drank it. But I never used it when drinking water was available. Nor did I feel any urge to use the coffee, tobacco, beer and wines which the Vietnamese gave us on about three special occasions a year—Christmas, their holiday Tet, and their Independence Day.

My parents were not sure about my abstinence, since I wrote asking them to send me a pound of coffee and a pound of tobacco in each package. The reason was that these were two of the few things the North Vietnamese would allow us to have from our own packages, and since so little of mine was getting through to me I decided to get the coffee and tobacco for the other men. The fellows knew I didn't use these things and it surprised some of them that I would ask for them. They started kidding me, "Your folks will really think you've gone to the dogs, Larry." "I don't think so," I replied. "They'll send it anyway. I know you guys really like coffee, and pipe tobacco means a lot to you, and anyway not much of what my folks are sending is getting through to me." The fellows were almost astounded when my parents sent that coffee and tobacco, knowing that I didn't use it myself, and it made a lot of points for my parents.

As regards the Word of Wisdom, my years in captivity had at least one good effect—not on me but on my younger brother. He had been smoking for several years. My parents told me that on the day they received word that I had been shot down my brother quit smoking and did not smoke again. During those years too my brother got his wife baptized into the Church. This all makes those seven years worth it.

When Latter-day Saints think of Church standards they are bound to think of tithing. This principle didn't apply in prison, of course, but I had an interesting experience in that connection which spanned the seven-year period.

Shortly before I got shot down I put five hundred dollars in my Book of Mormon, two hundred of which was for tithing. Seven years later, one of the first things I did when I got back to Burley, Idaho, was to ask my parents where my Book of Mormon was.

"It's with your books in one of your footlockers," they replied.

"Well, there were five hundred dollars in that book when I left," I said. "Let's see if it's still there."

When I picked the book up I felt it and said, "Yep, it's still here." Sure enough, I opened it and there were the five hundred dollars.

The book had been with my wife for two or three years and then had been taken up to my parents' home with other belongings of mine. Having their own Book of Mormon, my parents had no need to look into mine, and in fact no one had read my copy since it was returned. The Lord had taken care of his tithing money, which I now duly paid to the bishop at the earliest opportunity.

I mentioned attitudes a few pages back. POWs had a great opportunity to practice the Christian principle of forgiveness. Not that we thought too much about forgiving our enemy when he was going out of his way to make life miserable for us and even deliberately inflicting physical pain on us. Now that it's over, I can say that I feel no hatred in my heart for the North Vietnamese people nor for any individual I met there, though I despise and loathe their governmental system which prohibits freedom of thought and controls one's every act. I have been able to forgive those who persecuted and tortured me—they did it because they were soldiers and were ordered to do it. Evil leaders bear the blame and will one day receive the punishment.

It was less easy to forgive the Vietnamese authorities for what they did to my wife and parents. They did not release my name as a prisoner of war until four years after I was shot down and during that time my loved ones did not know for sure whether I was alive or dead. They received no mail of any kind from me for 4 years, just as for 4½ years I received none from them. The North Vietnamese held it all back.

Despite their not knowing absolutely, my parents never gave up hope. They lived on faith. They had good reasons for this, for I had been promised by a servant of the Lord that if I would live a good life I would be preserved. In the patriarchal blessing I mentioned previously, I was given this promise: "If you keep your mind and body free from the things the Lord has forbidden, you shall be returned again to your loved ones in case you have to serve in the armed forces . . . Wherever you go you shall be watched over by the powers of heaven, and if you do your part you shall be preserved until the Lord calls you home."

I think my folks assumed that I was living a good enough life to claim this promise, but they couldn't know for sure. Maybe I hadn't kept my part of the bargain. My friends have since told me that my mother and father never gave up hope, they always had faith I would come back. Another person who never gave up hope was Alfred Knight, the stake patriarch who had pronounced that patriarchal blessing on my head more than ten years before I was shot down.

That promise in my patriarchal blessing was a tremendous support to me in prison, a sustaining power especially in the dark days. I felt I had tried to do my part and that God would therefore honor the promise. The time at last came when I was released and returned to my loved ones. In the emotion-filled period of greeting, my parents embraced me and my father said, "Son, I'm proud of you."

I've thought since then that it may be like that in heaven for those who make it. Before we left there we received promises contingent on our conduct during mortality. I believe the Lord will have a great welcome in store for those who find their way back. I'm going to try to be one whom the Lord will greet with the words, "Well done!"

Chapter 8

BROTHERHOOD BEHIND BARS

I knew those two lines by Richard Lovelace long before I went to Vietnam. They're very well known.

"Stone walls do not a prison make,
Nor iron bars a cage."

These lines somehow mean more to me than they did before. We POWs felt that although the Vietnamese could lock us in their prisons they could not take our freedom from us. They could restrict our movement and a lot of other activities, but matters of the mind and the heart were still very much under our own control. We still had freedom of thought and, when not under torture, freedom of will. With this we were able as a group to maintain a very high morale.

I have already indicated some of the activities and attitudes which helped us to sustain morale. In the early days in particular, the system of communication between single or small cells was virtually indispensable. It occupied our time, kept us informed, stimulated a proper resistance to our captors, and encouraged us with the implicit reminder that each of us was part of a larger, concerned unit. In those days too our daily prayers and our scanty religious and patriotic services, conducted privately but simultaneously each Sunday, were strong sustainers of morale, as were the hard-won educational tidbits we were able to glean through our communication system. In the large room after November 1970, enhanced activities in these areas certainly helped to keep our morale at its peak.

It would all have been very difficult, I feel, but for the high caliber of the men I lived with in prison and their willingness to make whatever efforts and adjustments were necessary for us to get along together.

It would have been even better for us all if the North Vietnamese had rotated roommates every few months. That would have allowed us to meet new people, exchange experiences, get new ideas, learn varied subjects, and generally develop in personality. Being with a new roommate was frequently uplifting, and even when you shared the memories of past mistakes you helped each other. But rotation would have given us larger sources of information, and that alone would rule it out for our captors. In my case, I lived with only about sixty of the five hundred or so POWs held in North Vietnam.

When I first saw the size of the cells I would have to live in, I knew how vital it would be to have good roommates. When you are in a 9-foot by 3½-foot cell day and night with another person there is nowhere you can run away to, and if you don't get along well together you could live a life of complete frustration. Even if you do get along well it's no cinch to live at such close quarters when you have all the inconveniences of prison life. Since we have been released and the facts have become known, someone has made the comment that no marriage could ever endure under those cramped conditions.

One of my prayers in prison was that God would give me good roommates, and I must say that he answered this prayer completely. One and all, I felt and still feel a great affection and respect for those men I lived with, both in the smaller rooms and later in the forty-eight-man room. I believe they have the same feelings for me and that these will prove to be enduring friendships.

One thing that improved morale in the long-term when
we went into the large room was the implementation of U.S.
military discipline in ways previously impossible. This in itself
required an adjustment—whereas previously, when living solo
or in small groups, we had been fighting for ourselves all the
time against our captors, now we were being led by a senior
officer and could no longer fight for ourselves. He was our
representative with the enemy. Sometimes this would be
frustrating, and it took time to get used to it. This was one
reason it took three or four months to settle down completely
and have everything going smoothly.

We always knew who the senior officer was, and even
if sometimes some of us did not agree with the decision, we
did exactly what he ordered. Generally there was a rather
free association and we would address the senior officers by
their first names unless we were speaking in a military context
or in front of a North Vietnamese. Most of them preferred
this and it worked out well. It in no way diminished our
respect for them or the military discipline they represented.
The closeness of the group made it impractical to stand on
the usual military ceremony governed by differences of rank
—to always call senior officers "Sir," for example.

Naturally the North Vietnamese did not like our chain of
command under which the senior officer in the room ran
the room. Instead they tried to set up a system under which
junior officers would run the room. For a while they wouldn't
give us anything if we didn't ask for it through the junior
officers they had appointed, and in this way they deprived
us of things like soap, toothpaste, toilet paper, etc. All this
was embarrassing to the junior officers, who hadn't asked for
and certainly didn't want the appointment to run the rooms.
Though the withholding of supplies made things extremely inconvenient for us we adhered to the proper system of working
always through the senior officers except in cases of emergency
such as sickness, and finally the Vietnamese junior officer
program fell apart.

Actually the North Vietnamese never seemed to be able to sustain a program, either good or bad. Even programs aimed against the prisoners, whom in theory they had under their control, just seemed to fade out after a while.

When we moved into the large room in November 1970, we organized immediately in the military sense: the senior officer in command, four sections of twelve men each led by a flight commander, and duties allocated to each section on a rotational basis—sweeping the room, passing out the food, washing the dishes, and so on. But it took about six weeks before we all settled down to the point of organizing our activities and programs. For the most part we hadn't known each other previously, so first we spent time exchanging biographies and just generally getting to know each other. Then in January of 1971 we began the education courses and related activities I have described in chapter 6.

It would be an unreasoning idealization to suggest that all was constantly sweetness and light and that there was never the slightest difficulty between POWs in any of the rooms I lived in. In the cramped and physically unpleasant conditions it was easy to get irritated with each other when men were tired, when they were hungry, when they didn't have anything to do. As an illustration, one day Jerry Coffee and I got into an argument in our two-man, 9-by-3½-foot room. It started with talking about food. I was telling him about a restaurant I had heard about, a German-name restaurant above the city of Bountiful, Utah. Jerry asked: "What do you think the definition of *bountiful* is?" I told him it meant an abundance of one thing or another. Before we knew it we had gotten into an argument over the definition of *bountiful*, which is just about as silly as two people can get. It actually degenerated into name-calling. Of course, we were both sorry about it when we cooled down. It is a rather extreme example, too, as regards relationships with my roommates, for while we heard of other rooms having living-together problems, any difficulties we had in the rooms I lived in were very small by comparison.

The AP article I refer to in chapter 12 theorizes on the "violent clashes" between men caged like animals and the victims of constant frustration. This speculation is completely off the beam. There were of course arguments and disagreements, but I heard of only two examples where one man hit another in the entire 8½ years of POW living in North Vietnam. That's a pretty small percentage out of five hundred or so men and a million prison days.

Particularly in the large room, I am sure that our ability to get along well with each other had much to do with our entertainment and educational programs. We really were busily engaged in helping each other to learn. We may not have learned much of permanent value but the programs did help time pass without our becoming bored, without our becoming irritated with each other. Instead the programs promoted a cheerful comradeship. Our forty-eight-man group was probably the greatest group in the entire prison camp. Later I talked to men who had lived in all the other rooms at one time or another and we discussed what they and we had done with their time. Almost all of those I talked to were amazed that we had such an outstanding room.

I felt all the time that we were developing in maturity, of which getting along with people is an essential part. For all that, it was about four months before we had all adjusted completely to large-room living and things were running smoothly there. I was particularly interested to observe the adjustments made by myself and others I had lived with in small groups. It almost seemed that we made personality changes to meet the new circumstances.

Our morale was high too because we truly felt ourselves to be part of a unique fraternity or brotherhood. The North Vietnamese tried to break this down by methods designed to turn us against each other. One of their little tricks was to give one room some pencil and paper for a short period while still withholding it from another room. Another ploy was to let one man in a two-man room write a letter home but not the other man. By such means they hoped to make us bicker with each other. So far as I know it didn't work. When my roommate was allowed to write home I was glad for him although I was sorry I couldn't do it too. Given a choice, I know he would have let me write every other time.

We tried to be considerate of one another, not to be down on each other, or criticize each other, or say cutting things. Naturally we slipped sometimes, but I believe this negative kind of reaction was kept to an absolute minimum. On the positive side, acts of service and kindness, even at risk of punishment, were commonplace. When men were sick, roommates would give them their clothing to help them get warmer and stronger. Passing things to people in other rooms was forbidden and punishable, but we did it to help each other. If someone needed something, we tried to get it to him.

I can think of several examples. It was not common for the North Vietnamese deliberately to deprive a prisoner of food, but they would sometimes do it to weaken a man's resistance to their demands or to prison disciplines. On one occasion a man in a "solo" cell was being given this treatment, his food being cut down over a sustained period. To get food to him, another prisoner performed the difficult task of climbing up to the attic of the building, crawling all the way across the building till he was over the victim's cell, then lowering down to him bread saved from other men's meals. If he had been caught in this act of frustrating our captors' designs he would have been harshly punished. He did it because of his love and concern for a brother in the fraternity.

In the early days of my captivity, while my stomach was still of normal capacity, I used to have some bread left over. On the other hand, Col. Risner in the next cell to me had had his stomach stretched by the bulky food and needed more to eat. By arrangement over our communication system I carried my extra bread in my towel when I went to the bath area and left it there for him to pick up when it was his turn to wash. He got a couple of loaves this way before I was moved from that building.

After November 1970, the man I referred to in chapter 5—the man with the tremendous will to live whose arm and hand were in such a bad way—was in Camp Unity in one of the other large rooms. A major concern was how to retain whatever life remained in the fingers on the afflicted hand, immobile as they were, in the hope that something could be done for them when he eventually returned to the United States. For this purpose they needed to be bent back and forth in daily exercise. This was too painful for him to do it himself, but he could stand it if someone did it for him.

Several prisoners lent their assistance to this important project, but one in particular more or less took upon himself the duties of therapist. Every day for an hour or more at a time he would sit with the injured man on the edge of the island which was our bedspace, patiently massaging the afflicted fingers and bending them back and forth. To him it was no casual thing but a matter of major concern—the welfare of an injured comrade.

A dramatic example of assistance to a man in need occurred in our forty-eight-man room, where instead of the bucket we had an improved though still rudimentary "toilet facility" just inside the door. One of the men in our room had a denture with one front tooth on it, and one night when he was sick he ejected his denture while throwing up in the "toilet." One of the other men went in and thrust his arm down up to the shoulder in the malodorous pile and felt around until he had retrieved the denture. That's the type of man I had the honor to live with in prison.

With so many willing to give, one minor problem sometimes was how to be a gracious receiver. There's an art to this, and having been taught all our lives to be independent it wasn't easy to learn it. So in our eight-man room we finally drew up some ground rules. They went something like this: First, don't offer somebody something unless you want him to have it. Second, if somebody offers you something and you want it, say "Thank you" and take it. Don't play around and say: "Well, I really don't want it. You need it worse than

I do." It has already been determined that the person wants to give it to you, so go ahead and take it if you want it. Third, if you really don't want what you are offered, just say, "No, thank you, I don't want it." But don't decline the offer just because you think it's the right thing to do. These ground rules worked very smoothly.

Being able to put something over on our captors was always a great morale-builder. Naturally we appropriated whatever we could from them and cached it. We usually had a spare razor-blade or two around. Another item we managed to relieve our guards of was whitewash. We could use this for ink, writing on dark surfaces. We stole pencils from our guards, but couldn't keep them in that form for fear of discovery. So we broke open the wood, removed the lead, and distributed it in pieces for men to hide in the seams of their clothing. We could also write somewhat with the lead in the toothpaste tubes by rolling part of a tube tightly, biting it into a point, and breaking a piece off to expose another part when the lead in the "point" was exhausted.

Particularly in the large room we improvised rather freely in making ink, using medicines (latterly, when we could get a few) or combining water with such things as charcoal, dirt, or brick dust. For writing paper we would use some of what was given us for toilet paper. Using bamboo pens we had made, we would write our own little booklets for the language classes, music classes, and so forth.

Night time was the best time to write, because then we would be less likely to be caught. Once the guard had locked the door for the last time—about 5:00 P.M.—and everything had settled down we would get under our mosquito nets where the Vietnamese couldn't see us and write by the light of the single 40-watt bulb which "illuminated" our large room day and night. Sometimes we would spend all night for two or three nights making copies of the booklets, trying to get caught up, only to have them discovered and removed in the Vietnamese inspections. In these unheralded visits they wouldn't look for guns or clubs or any kind of weapon—they well knew we had none of those. They looked for our educational information and took it away from us. But they never could discourage us. Always we would just bounce back and start writing again.

Of the many intangible things which kept our morale high I would place high on the list our conviction that we had kept the faith. It was not a matter for heroics—we didn't think of ourselves as heroes in any case, but just as ordinary Americans caught up in unusual circumstances and trying to do what duty and conscience required of us. The fact that we had made disclosures to the enemy under physical duress was to every one of us lamentable, and in the first instance often overwhelming in the remorse each felt. But gradually, through our communication system, we came to realize that we were not alone in this, that others had similarly had to give way, and that doing so finally under the irresistible pressure of prolonged physical torment did not in fact signify an individual weakness of will or lack of courage. As I have indicated before, we bounced back with unbroken spirit, ready for the battle with guards and circumstances which was our daily lot.

By looking after each other as best we could, by being loyal to each other, we kept faith with each other. But for this, nothing else would have mattered much. We kept faith with God. And we kept faith with our country. There were exceptions, but they were few.

I have been told many times since returning home that the POW issue has united the country again. I would like to hope that that is true, that in our small way we have stimulated this unity. We former POWs love our country. We had many years to think about it, and the expressions of love and loyalty for our country made as we arrived back group by group in this great land reflect the sober thoughts and the earnest feelings of those years.

Maintaining a unity of purpose and attitude in a large democratic country is bound to be difficult. To do this a country needs to be welded together in a good cause. In a sense the communist countries have it easier. The North Vietnamese soldiers in particular have been pumped up with propaganda to the effect that they have a great cause, a cause worth dying for. Having no other source of information, they believe it. Our own democratic society does not indoctrinate military personnel as to a political theory or system, so in many respects our young men going to war do not understand what they are fighting for. In these circumstances, when communists capture them it is perhaps not too difficult to change their ideas.

The POWs in North Vietnam were older and had more experience and basic maturity. Even though I'm sure that, in the absence of proper sources of information, all of us at times wondered to some extent just where right and wrong lay in the issues, I believe that in the long run we all felt the U.S. policy to be right. Certainly it is difficult to evaluate our success or failure in the Vietnam War, and I am not setting out to do so here. If a person believes we lost, he can find enough influential, important writers and speakers to prove the point. If one believes we won, he can adduce influential voices to demonstrate that conclusion. Perhaps time will reveal the true picture, and perhaps not.

However that may be, in prison we had no argument with what our government was doing to get us released. We knew that there were political facts to be faced, and that our government was doing all it could properly do to secure our release from an enemy who had no regard for human life or dignity and who treated us (and their own nationals who were POWs in South Vietnam) as pawns in the game.

Consequently, so far as I know none of us either expected or wanted a "release at any price" policy, a sacrifice of U.S. honor just to get us home. When it was reported that a high U.S. official had said, "A handful of prisoners cannot dictate the foreign policy of this government," every prisoner I talked to agreed with that statement. We didn't want our circumstances to dictate policy. Although we longed to come home we knew we couldn't and we knew why. We all realized that our lives were expendable. We were willing to wait—to die, if necessary. After all, when you go to war there's a chance you'll be killed. Many of my friends made that sacrifice in the Vietnam War. To my mind they were fighting in a worthwhile cause, combating the forces of darkness and horror represented by communism. In that sense they were defending the best that is in our way of life, the cause of freedom. Had we prisoners been called upon to die for that same cause I believe that few if any would not have been proud to do so.

Morale is a matter of mind and heart more than of circumstances. As prisoners we were members of a unique brotherhood; we were united against our captors; and we were loyal to the best that was in us. This unity engaged the mind and the heart on a high plane and helped us to overcome the unpleasant surroundings and overlook each other's human failings. Best of all, it kept uppermost in the mind and heart the memory of all that America meant to us. Someday, God willing, we would walk again in freedom in that wonderful land.

Chapter 9

TOWARD THE LIGHT

When 1970 dawned I was still in Camp Hope, near the city of Son Tay, living in a room with seven other men. As I indicated in Chapter 3, the worst years were now behind us. We began to see a little improvement in the food, for example; we got a little canned meat or fish now and again, and first thing each morning we now received some bread, which shortened the hunger pangs of the night. Getting outside every three or four days for an hour or two at a time gave us a little more fresh air and sunshine. Spurred particularly by the vitamins in the packages from home which the North Vietnamese were now allowing us to receive, our health began to pick up generally.

Why did we get improved conditions after October 1969? I believe there were two major reasons for this. One was the letter-writing campaign in America, in which hundreds of thousands addressed letters to Hanoi demanding an improvement in our conditions. Even though they wouldn't admit it, I believe this concerted effort impressed the North Vietnamese government. The second pressure on them was the International Red Cross conference held in Istanbul in September 1969, at which the situation of the American POWs was the principal subject of discussion.

Apparently the pressures were responsible also for the release of POW names. Even so the North Vietnamese could not bring themselves to make a full disclosure by publishing a complete list of the POWs in their hands. Instead it was made known that any American family concerned about whether a loved one was a POW in North Vietnam should write to that government's delegation in Paris, the site of the apparently interminable cease-fire negotiations. My parents wrote there and in April 1970 received confirmation that I was indeed alive in North Vietnam. Only that government knows why they did not spare my loved ones, and the loved ones of many other prisoners, the suffering of those years of uncertainty.

Now that my name was released, I was allowed to send and receive an occasional letter. I wrote my first POW letter to my wife in December 1969, though it was not delivered until after my name had been released. I first received a letter from home in August 1970. My parents received the first letter from me in July, one I had written in March or April. I had received the first package from home in February 1969, the second in September of that year. Packages arrived sporadically thereafter though, as with those for the other POWs, our captors always determined which of the contents I was allowed to have.

The term *letter* as used in the previous paragraph is not very descriptive. The number of letters was restricted both ways and each way we were allowed about six lines of writing per "letter." A card counted as a letter. A Christmas card I received from my children simply had their names written on it (obviously the accompanying letter had been removed). From the summer of 1970 until February 1973 I received some fourteen or fifteen of such "letters." My parents received four from me; my wife, six or seven.

While blessedly there were no more torture sessions to face after 1969, prison brutality was not completely at an end. It was as if the prison authorities were reluctant to relinquish entirely their "right" to control by force and physical violence.

They had to keep reminding us that they had the big guns. So periodically, clear up to about the end of 1972, they would take a prisoner out where the rest of us could hear or see and beat on him. They did this on several occasions. One night they took a man out because he had made an American flag. In their barbaric way they beat him and cracked some ribs, then broke an eardrum by beating him on the face and head.

The conditions at Camp Hope were very poor, even in comparison to the other prisons we had been in. The windows were about 4 inches high and 2½ feet wide and were always shuttered, leaving us with almost no fresh air to breathe. The cells were unlit by day and poorly lit by a low-powered light bulb at night. The food was very bad. Rats ran around freely. Until the end of 1969 too there was always the possible threat of more torture. And to make it worse, we almost never got outside until late October 1969, despite the fact that there was a big compound available which we could have exercised in.

We all heartily longed to get away from this camp. I personally prayed to the Lord consistently, asking him somehow to grant us better living conditions, and I know my roommates offered prayers to the same end. The answer to those prayers caused me some subsequent reflections about answers to prayer generally.

I've mentioned previously the difficulty I had in learning to fly and the fervent prayers I offered in seeking the Lord's help to get my wings. The prayers were answered. I got the wings. Later I received flight orders assigning me to Vietnam, as a result of which I fell into North Vietnamese hands. What would have happened had I prayed differently back at Webb AFB—if I had asked that God's will be done in the matter? Perhaps I would not have become a pilot, in which case the years 1966-1973 presumably would have been very different.

After praying continually at Camp Hope for better conditions, we were moved on July 14, 1970, to another camp

MOCK-UP DESIGN OF CAMP HOPE (AUTHOR LIVED IN TALLEST BUILDING SHOWN)

"AERIAL" VIEW OF CAMP HOPE MOCK-UP

which was nearer to Hanoi, Camp Faith. Here we did have better conditions. Was that the best answer to our prayers, or should we have left the details to the Lord? Who can tell? All we know is that in November 1970, four months after we left Camp Hope, it was raided by U.S. Commandos. Had we still been there we probably would have been liberated 2½ years earlier than we were.

But life is full of such "what ifs?" Meanwhile I was now at Camp Faith in a room with eleven others. Here we had more space per man, more air circulating in the room. We even had a small table in the room plus a shelf-like arrangement where we could put whatever the camp authorities would let us have out of our packages. At this point I had been in captivity more than four years, and this was the first room I had lived in which contained any furniture at all.

The raid on Son Tay had excellent effects for us POWs. The Green Berets didn't get us out but they got us together, and that made the raid a success. It scared the North Vietnamese and forced them to bring all the prisoners back to Hanoi. Our total number was now so large that they did not have smaller rooms available for us and much against their will they were obliged to put us in big rooms. I was put in a room in Camp Unity with fifty-six other men. This gave us a bedspace width of only seventeen inches per man to sleep in, but we didn't care about that. At last we were close together, at last we were in a big group. That was the important thing.

We moved in in late November of 1970. Just before Christmas the camp authorities conducted a big inspection, a harassment-type inspection. At this time they took everything that was American, all the little things they had previously allowed us to have from the packages which had got through from our loved ones. We lost all of our soap, our toothbrushes, all clothing that was American—everything. We were pretty down in the dumps on Christmas Day 1970. Nevertheless we had a Christmas program that evening as planned.

Between Christmas and New Years nine men were moved out, leaving forty-eight men in the room. We now had twenty-one inches apiece to sleep in. It wasn't exactly a king-size bed but it was enough. We were happier than we had ever been in North Vietnam. The room measured approximately sixty feet by twenty-four feet. A narrow strip of floor about two feet wide on the long sides and four feet on the short sides ran all around the outer edge of the room, surrounding the concrete island in the center which comprised the major portion of the room. We slept on our rush mats on this island. The long sides were each raised about eighteen to twenty inches off the floor at the outer edge and slanted slightly upwards from there to meet a central, foot-wide shelf running the length of the island. We slept twenty-four men on each side, most of the time with no boards between each man's thin mat and the concrete. (We varied by one or two men from time to time, but the total stayed basically at forty-eight for the rest of the time I was in this camp.)

The room had five windows, two on the north side and three on the south. True to form, the camp authorities kept the three south windows covered with mats, thereby restricting air circulation. Even at that, the air supply here was a vast improvement on any prison room we had previously lived in.

There were about nine rooms in this camp, each of them slightly different from the others yet all of the same basic pattern. I am describing the one I was in. We had no furniture whatsoever—no tables, no chairs. At mealtimes the end men would roll their mats back and we would put the food containers on the end of the island. We would dish out the food and each man would come along and pick up his bowl and plate and spoon and take them to his own bedspace, holding them in his hand as he ate.

This room had an advantage over some of the others in the block in that it had a semi-toilet bath area off the main room. While it was still primitive, it was a little more convenient than the buckets we had been using most of the time

I had been a prisoner. In this room, too, we had a water tank that we would fill daily from the courtyard cistern, giving us water to wash our hands.

We had two loudspeakers in our room. They played Vietnamese programs, propaganda programs written by the North Vietnamese press for our benefit. Most of the men just ignored them. The poor-quality speakers turned you off anyway. As I indicated previously, now and then American music would be played in an attempt to gain our interest preparatory to the main program.

By late summer of 1971 it was obvious to the North Vietnamese government that serious negotiations were going on for a cease-fire in South Vietnam. This meant that the POWs would have to be released in the not-too-distant future. This thinking may have been the reason that after July that year we had an addition made to our daily fare—hot milk with our morning bread. This helped to put back some of the flesh we had lost and certainly was a dietary improvement.

In November 1970 or shortly after that we began to be allowed outside for a few hours each day. We got out for about two hours in the morning to wash ourselves, eat, wash our dishes, wash our clothes, or whatever else we had to do. We would also get out for an hour to an hour and a half each afternoon, except Sundays. It was very pleasant to be out in the sunshine for a change. In the very small courtyard space allocated to our forty-eight men we set aside a section for sunbathers. Usage was organized on a rotation basis, each man getting his turn in the sun every few days. For the sake of health we tried to get in the sun as much as we could.

I lived in the large room in Camp Unity at Hanoi Hilton for eighteen months. On May 13, 1972, 209 prisoners were moved from Hanoi to a camp near the Chinese border. Why, we didn't know. We were told it was to protect us from the U.S. bombing of Hanoi. Perhaps the real reason was to get us well to the North in case, provoked by North Vietnamese tactics at the bargaining table, the U.S. should make some large-scale effort to rescue the POWs. I have described in chapter 4 the nightmare truck ride this journey involved and which I experienced to the extent of two round trips. For all practical purposes the remainder of our time in captivity was spent in this northern camp.

This camp had just about all the qualities of a dungeon except that it was not underground. The walls were built of stone and, like the floors, were always wet. The windows were very small, the cells always dark. In the evening we would get a two-inch kerosene candle to light the room.

The camp authorities let us know that earnest talks were in progress between the U.S. and North Vietnam that could result in a cease-fire in South Vietnam and in our being returned home. Naturally, the news they gave us of the progress of the negotiations was colored in their favor and designed to cause us discouragement. From time to time they would tell us in detail what position their side was taking, what their negotiators had said, and so on, dismissing the U.S. case by a sentence such as, "The American side brought out again their shop-worn arguments." They were particularly concerned to tell us when the talks were not going well. They told us on Halloween morning, 1972, that the talks had broken down on October 8, but we were encouraged by the obvious fact that the camp authorities were unhappy about the breakdown. If it upset the North Vietnamese, our side must be doing the right thing, we felt.

Although the talks had fallen through, the setback was only temporary. The enemy could see that the time of our repatriation was not far distant, so some more concessions were in order. In late October or early November they began letting us have writing materials (the first time we got these on a general basis in our entire period of imprisonment) and a magazine or two which had been confiscated from previous packages. In our room we got a couple of three-year-old sports magazines!

We knew that we would not be returned to Hanoi until the bombing there stopped and that President Nixon would not stop the bombing until an agreement had been reached in the Paris negotiations. So despite the trying conditions of the truck journey our morale was very high as we traveled back to Hanoi on January 20, 1973. We knew then that in effect we were on the way home.

That light at the end of the tunnel, so long a mere pinpoint, was about to burst into noontide brilliance. For me, only twenty-three days of captivity remained. It was remarkable what a sudden improvement there was in prison conditions during that time. Now for the first time in our prison life we actually got out into the courtyard in big groups, meeting with prisoners we previously had known only by name and reputation through our communication system. Now we were allowed to play volleyball. Now the camp authorities and guards actually tried to be nice to us. They even gave us some American magazines and a few books to read—some of our own reading material they had held back from our packages.

A requirement of the Paris agreement was that all captives were to be read the text of the agreement within five days of the signing. The North Vietnamese read this text to us on January 30, three days after the signing, and gave us copies. The agreement required that all the U.S. prisoners be released in four fifteen-day increments, the sick and injured being released first and the others following in order of "seniority" in prison—that is, first in, first out. At long last the dream was coming true. Each man could now know roughly when he would get home.

About February 9, the Vietnamese handed out to us the letters we had previously received from home and read. (We had never been allowed to keep letters—just to read each for a few minutes when received, then hand it back.) Curiously, with these older letters some of us received other letters from home which we had not before seen. This was undoubtedly an administrative error on the part of our captors since it proved conclusively, when we were within a couple of days of freedom, that they had held our letters up as a matter of policy. At this time I received five or six new letters from home. One of them told me of the death of President David O. McKay, which had taken place in January 1970.

On February 11 we were all locked up for the night and some of us were standing up in the window looking out into the bare courtyard—the mats having been removed from the windows at the time the partitions were taken down in the courtyard. As we watched, Col. Risner, accompanied by two guards, emerged from the building in which the "quizzes" were held and began going around, stopping at each room and calling up into the window. When he got to our room he called up to me.

"Larry, ask Major Runyan to come to the window."

Major Runyan was the senior ranking officer in our room. When he arrived in the window, Col. Risner gave him the good news. The first group of POWs would be released the following day if everything went well. In preparation we would get our "going-away" clothes on the night of the eleventh.

I was scheduled for release in the first group. For some reason I didn't sleep much that night.

Chapter 10

RETURNED TO LIFE

February 12, 1973, was a beautiful day in North Vietnam —at least to 112 American POWs. We had received our "going-away" clothes the night before—blue slacks, a light blue shirt, a windbreaker, shoes and socks. (We had these clothes for about twelve hours in all.) We swept our rooms and cleaned them as well as we could, then packaged up the blankets, clothing, and other things we were not bringing away with us, leaving everything as tidy as possible. We guessed the Vietnamese would later claim that we left the prison in a dirty condition. Sure enough, they did.

For "old time's sake" I brought a set of my gear out. I brought black pajamas, tire sandals, some of the other clothing we wore in prison, a cup, a toothbrush, and toothpaste. Later I gave them to the Wright Patterson Air Force Museum.

When the time came to leave, the 112 men assembled in the courtyard and made their way under guard to the gate of Hanoi Hilton. This was the first time we had moved any-where from Hanoi Hilton without being blindfolded and handcuffed. Outside the gate six buses awaited us—this time we were to travel first-class. We loaded onto the buses and they pulled away. I looked back at the closed gate and the grim expanse of wall and barbed wire. It had been six years, nine months, and six days since I first saw Hanoi Hilton, twenty-one days after being captured.

I was on bus number five with nineteen other men. Following the first four buses it made off in the direction of Gia Lam airport, which is three or four miles out of Hanoi. Near the airport the buses stopped and we got out at a building where we were to await the arrival of the U.S. planes that would take us home. Here we were each given a sandwich, and those who wanted it received a bottle of Hanoi beer. The contents of the sandwich intrigued and amused us. We would have supposed that, consistent with their recent efforts to cosy up to us, the North Vietnamese would have given us something attractive for the last meal in their country. But at least it was memorable—the sandwich contained the same old pig fat we had been eating during all our years in prison.

We reboarded the buses and soon arrived at the airport. There we saw a beautiful sight—a United States C-141 aircraft sitting out there on the runway with a big American flag on its tail. The first two buses went over to the aircraft and we watched with eager anticipation as they unloaded and friends and comrades disappeared into the plane.

When the third bus made no move, we began to express some sense of urgency at their delay. We had an English-speaking guard in our bus, and he responded by telling us the plane was loaded. "Baloney!" I said. "That plane will hold all 112 of us. Let's go and get on it!" "No," he replied, "that one is loaded. Here comes another one now."

If a stationary C-141 was a beautiful sight to us on the runway, how shall I describe the elegant bird the second one was as it flew beneath a deck of white clouds, circled around, and landed? In the emotion of the moment I could readily accept that it was the loveliest sight I had ever seen. As it landed, the first one took off. The next two busloads boarded the second aircraft. "That plane is loaded too," said the guard. "Maybe there will be another one."

We hoped so. In a few minutes the third aircraft appeared in view, flying under the overcast and as good-looking

as the other two. As the second one took off, this one landed
and taxied in. Our bus and the one following us drove out to
the flight line.

Awaiting us was an American military commission. How
good it was to see those United States uniforms again! We
got out of the bus and marched in military style up to the
waiting officers. A Vietnamese officer—the one we knew as
Rabbit—read off our names one by one as we saluted Col.
Al Lynn, the U.S. colonel in charge. He shook each of us
by the hand. Beyond him was another colonel who talked
to us briefly. Then a U.S. military escort walked us to the
plane, giving some of us a hug of welcome as they did so.

What a tremendous experience it was to walk onto that
airplane! After all the years of waiting and hoping, it didn't
seem possible that the day we had dreamed of had really
come. The 112 who left that day included Lt. j.g. Everett
Alvarez, the first to be captured in North Vietnam, 8½ years
a POW; Col. Robinson Risner, nearly 7½ years, the first
American to make contact with me in Hanoi Hilton nearly
seven years previously; Navy Lt. Gerald L. Coffee, 7 years,
and Lt. j.g. William M. Tschudy, 7¾ years, both former
roommates of mine; Major Sam Johnson, who was shot down
with me; and many others I had come to love and respect
while a POW. Their thoughts and emotions must have been
much like mine as they walked onto the plane that would
fly them to freedom.

We were met at the door by three pretty young ladies,
the first American girls we had seen in years. They were
attractively dressed, well groomed, and smelled delightfully
of perfume. We sat down in the seats and looked around.
Everything seemed like heaven. Just like heaven. When the
back doors of that C-141 closed there were tears in the eyes
of every man aboard.

It took us approximately 3½ hours to fly from Gia Lam
to Clark AFB in the Philippines. We touched down without
delay and started unloading from the airplane. Like most of

the other men my eyes were still red as we walked to the back of the airplane to deplane. Walking just in front of me was Major Sam Johnson. I said to him, "Sam, I'm not going to cry, I'm not going to cry." But when I got to the back of the airplane and looked out of the window and saw all the people there, I said, "Sam, I think I'm going to cry." His eyes too were moist as he smiled at me in reply.

There were perhaps a thousand people to greet us, and as we walked down the ramp one at a time we heard them clapping, singing, and cheering in welcome. I didn't start crying until after I had saluted and shaken hands with the admiral and the general, who greeted us on the red carpet laid out for us. Between the bottom of the ramp and the two officers was a civilian Pentagon official—President Nixon's number one assistant on POW affairs, I discovered later, and a very fine person. As I told him my name, he threw his arms around me. "My name is Roger Shields," he said. "I'm LDS, Larry, and your father is a friend of mine, and he asked me to give you a hug." And he did.

As we walked down that red carpet toward the waiting buses and heard the little children chanting, "Welcome home! Welcome home!" like a cheerleading rally at a football game, I could no longer contain the tears. Nor could the other men. Nearly everyone on my bus was crying again. One of the men turned to me and said: "Larry, the thing that makes this so great is that you know those people out there mean it. They're not here to see us because we're freaks, they're here to see us because they love us." "You're right," I replied, "that's exactly why they're here." The welcome at Clark was an extremely humbling and moving experience.

At Clark we were assigned beds in the hospital, where doctors checked our general physical condition. I can't describe the ecstasy of that first shower, the sheer joy of feeling hot water coursing over my body; then, with a body which felt truly clean for the first time since 1966, putting on clean clothes. My planeload was on the fourth floor of the hospital; the first group was on the floor above us. We were all extremely keyed up; we didn't sleep for about three days, getting maybe an hour or so a night. Sleeping in a bed with a mattress and sheets was going to take a little getting used to.

What we lost in sleep we certainly made up in food. It was good to eat with a knife and fork again. For our first meal in freedom we had steak or chicken, corn on the cob, strawberry shortcake and ice cream, all in huge quantities. I gained six pounds in those three days. We were burning up energy and eating like horses. I was told that the 112 of us ate forty gallons of ice cream the first night.

I was assigned an "escort officer," Capt. Richard Mallchok, whose job was to help me ease back into normal life. We discussed changes which had taken place on the American scene since 1966 and what adjustments these would mean for me. He gave me some personal news, both good and bad. He also did all the necessary legwork for me, getting me clothes, bags, shaving gear, and so forth—all the things most of us take for granted and which I would need to start life again.

At Clark we all phoned our families in the States. I heard my parents' voices for the first time since December 1965, and this was another great emotional experience.

I had found out in 1972 that my wife had divorced me and remarried while I was in prison. The talk with my parents added some detail I had not known and sharpened again the sense of loss and the feeling of concern about my two dear children. Most of the other returned POWs would be returning to wife and children in a few days but this joy was not to be mine. I was sad and very sorry for myself at my loss—demoralized, I might almost say.

Fortunately for me I met Col. George Kiser soon after making the phone call. An air force dentist, he was the president of the LDS branch at Clark and became a source of great comfort to me at this trying time. I went to meet him, and we sat in the hallway in his reception area. I could tell right away that he was a good man; it just radiated from him. As we talked about my problem we were both weeping, ignoring the glances of the waiting patients.

"Larry," Col. Kiser was saying, "I have been praying for weeks that I would know what to tell you. I knew a little of your situation and I knew you would be coming through here and I wanted to have something to say that would ease your sorrow. But," he added, "I don't know what to tell you."

"Well," I responded, "I'm a little bitter. I don't know whether God answers prayers any more. All the time I was away I prayed that God would take care of my family for me, and it doesn't seem as if he has."

George Kiser wouldn't have that. "Larry, you have no right to judge God," he insisted, "you have no right." And then he sort of chastised me for my attitude. He was right, and I knew it.

As he got up to leave, he said: "I've just thought of something. I have a true story I want you to read. It will help you. I'll bring it up to your room tonight and let you read it."

"Okay," I said, "thank you."

That night he brought up to my room a book called *No More Strangers*,[1] which contains several personal accounts of conversions to the gospel. One story is by Irving Cohen, a Jewish fellow who lost his wife and his little girl through divorce because he had joined the Church. It tells how the Lord rewarded his faithfulness with another wife and a much larger family, and how even his daughter came to him after sixteen years of separation. "You read that story four or five times and spend some time on your knees," Col. Kiser said, "and see if that doesn't do something to help your spirit."

I did read the story several times and pray, and it helped me very much. It lifted my spirit. It prompted me to decide that there is no profit in being sad, especially about what you can't change. One has to go on living, and he might as well

---

[1]By Hartman and Connie Rector, published 1971 by Bookcraft.

be happy about it. My problem was not of my making and was uncorrectable, so I must resolve to pick up again and do the best I could.

George Kiser was a great inspiration to me and did a tremendous amount to strengthen my faith in God. He encouraged me to continue to pray and ask for guidance, which I did. With this, and the reading of Irving Cohen's story, I felt as if a load had been lifted from my mind and heart, and there came to my soul a sense of peace, an assurance that everything would work out right. I don't know how this will come about but I know that it will.

During my short stay at Clark I met other Church members, and I attended a meeting of the branch presidency and their families at the hospital where I bore my testimony of the gospel and gave a short talk on my experiences in prison. This was the first of many occasions when I would have such an opportunity. At this point the majority of the POWs were still in Hanoi. So as not to jeopardize their position in any way, not until the last man was home did I or other returned POWs mention in our speeches anything about the torture and other bad treatment we had received. This was a condition the returned POWs voluntarily observed to safeguard their comrades who had not yet been released.

While I was at Clark we returned POWs received letters by the thousands from young people. Those I received are among my most treasured possessions, showing as they do the true feelings of these youngsters. Many of them were very moving. One that particularly touched my heart was from an eleven-year-old boy. It showed a deep concern for us, a simple faith, and a gratitude for finally receiving an answer to his prayers. I believe that little boy's letter meant more to me than any other letter I received during those first weeks after my release. The letter read:

"Dear Sir,

"I sure am glad your all done with that war. I said a prayer every night for all the men to be released and

—*Air Force photo*

RETURNED POW CHESLEY ADMIRES SCHOOL CHILDREN'S VALENTINE'S DAY
DISPLAY AT CLARK AFB

it finally came true. Welcome home sir. I would have gave my life to get you guys out of there but I don't think my parents would like it. I think you'll like being home with your families. I'm a six grader."

After five days at Clark, I left with other former POWs en route for Travis AFB, California. Six other planes had left previously. I was on "lucky" number seven—fog prevented us from landing at Travis, and we were rerouted to Alameda Naval Air Station at Oakland. A crowd had driven over there and they gave us a tremendous welcome. From Alameda we went by bus to Travis, where we were met by the TV cameras.

At Travis my parents were waiting to greet me. There is no way to describe this meeting. I can only say that it was probably the greatest emotional experience of my life. We embraced and wept together. It had indeed been a long and trying time for them.

In my private room at the hospital we exchanged family confidences and learned more about each other's ordeal. They explained that although they had never given up hope during the four years before my name was released by the North Vietnamese, my wife had thought me to be dead. It was still hard to take, but I began to understand more about the reasons prompting the divorce. Certainly it was not easy for anyone left in the position JoDene was in. I have no malice or hard feelings toward her.

At Travis I met the LDS chaplain assigned to the hospital, Crozier Fitzgerald. He was determined to see that my life would not be dull any longer. I arrived on Saturday, February 17, and the following day was the stake conference in nearby Napa Stake. At that conference I was asked to bear my testimony, which I did. I think it was effective. I feel that I do have a strong testimony of the gospel, and people have responded to this in the various Church gatherings I have spoken in.

I received the sacrament that Sunday for the first time since 1966. What a blessing it was to make that renewal of covenants! As I took the bread and water I asked the Lord to wipe away the sins I had committed. Only the day before, I had put on temple garments again, which my father had brought to Travis. Here was another great blessing—to have again the strength and protection of that special garment. With this and the sacrament I felt a keen sense of recommittal to God's will.

Chaplain Fitzgerald introduced me to a young lady who later took me to a concert. In the middle of the concert the music stopped and the conductor went to the microphone. "Tonight we have an honored guest in our midst," she said. "Would Captain Larry Chesley please stand up." I stood, and the audience applauded. After a while I sat down; they continued to clap so I stood up again. The applause seemed to go on for several minutes, but they finally quit and I sat down.

Now the conductor said: "We know what Captain Chesley's favorite song is, and even though this lady has never before sung it in public she has consented to sing it for Captain Chesley tonight." At that Susan Ruesch sang the song "Somewhere, My Love" from the movie *Dr. Zhivago*. I had first heard the song in prison—some American music prelude to a propaganda program—and I thought it very beautiful.

It was like that all the time I stayed in California. People seemed very anxious to honor the returned POWs wherever I went—the performance of the BYU dancers, a Laurel-Explorer dance, a little-theatre group. I had speaking engagements too at meetings and firesides throughout the Sacramento area, where I bore my testimony to the people of the Church and told them a little bit about my life in prison. It was all a very humbling experience. Everyone was so kind.

While I was at Travis I made a lot of friends among Church members in the area, and I continually had friends

CAPTAIN CHESLEY GETS TO KNOW HIS CHILDREN, DEBBIE AND DON

coming up to see me. I had a lot of phone calls too. The other returned POWs jocularly expressed some envy at this— I was the most popular guy on the floor, they said. They and the nurses were greatly impressed by the way the Church members contacted me and kept in touch. I remember my debriefer, Don Hartman, saying, "Well, I was supposed to keep you entertained, but you're doing it for me." Don and I did a lot of things together; we went to some dances and plays and parties and other social gatherings. He's not LDS, but I got him some dates with nice LDS girls, with the thought that in that way he might get interested in the Church. We had a good time together.

On March 7 I flew to Salt Lake City, where by invitation I spoke briefly to the Utah House of Representatives then in session. Here as everywhere else there seemed to be a great stirring of patriotic feeling around the matter of the returning POWs I was honored to be representing.

It was in Salt Lake City that day that I met my two children Debbie and Don, seven years and three months to the day since I had kissed them goodbye. Debbie was now eleven, Don nine. No one will need any explanation as to my feelings at that meeting. As to how the children felt, Debbie said it well when asked if she remembered me. "I don't remember him," she replied, "but I still love him."

This simple statement could almost be the keynote to the return of the 589 POWs. The nation gave us a wonderful welcome. People did not remember us individually, but they still loved us. That made it all worth while.

Chapter 11

LOCAL BOY COMES HOME

"Silent weeping and prayer, hearty laughter and singing mixed as the heart of everyone swelled with love for his country, his God, and his men in uniform."

So wrote Janet Feiler in the *South Idaho Press* for March 12, 1973. The headlines for her article read: "Thousands Line Streets. Cheers, Tears Welcome Captain Chesley Home."

On March 10, 1973, the citizens of Burley, Idaho, and surrounding regions put on a magnificent welcome for the local boy who was fortunate enough to come home. Of all the official welcomes I received, this was by far the greatest in its scope. It was also the most moving for me, being staged in the community where I had spent my childhood and whose scenes and people had been among the foremost of my recollections in prison. It was a profoundly humbling experience.

Burley police estimated that the parade route was lined by thirty thousand people, some of whom had come hundreds of miles for the occasion. The hour-long parade contained over fifteen hundred persons in about a hundred entries comprising military units, high school bands and drill teams, children's groups, families, and businesses. It was led by a military honor guard, followed by a firetruck from which my two children and myself smiled and waved to that wonderful cheering crowd.

Star Ward Float (above) and Author with
Children in Burley Parade

Shortly we three left the parade and mounted a reviewing stand, where we joined my parents and several civic and military officials. From there I watched with a lump in my throat as military units passed by saluting, sign-holding children sang, danced, and threw candy kisses, bands played, and scores of vehicles drove by carrying "Welcome Home" signs. I was glad to observe that in a position of honor near the front of the parade, riding in specially marked vehicles, were the families of men who had not been as fortunate as I and had fallen in the Vietnam War.

The scriptures tell us to pray about everything that is good, and I prayed to the Lord with all my heart that he would make my homecoming beautiful, particularly that it would be good weather for the parade and the watching crowds. When the parade started, the sun was shining. When it ended there was a little wind, and this was blowing hard by the time the program in the high school was over. That night two inches of snow fell. I was very grateful that we had beautiful parade weather for those who had done so much to make the day enjoyable.

It was obvious that our little community had turned out in full force and in addition people had come from all over the neighboring valleys to do me honor. Burley is not a big city, but they had planned on this program for a long time. A lot of people did a great deal of work to make it possible, and I felt very thankful to them. It was truly heartwarming and gratifying to me that so many people put forth the efforts they did to come and to make it such an inspiring occasion.

That afternoon Burley put on a special program in the high school gymnasium. There were approximately twenty-five hundred people present. Following welcoming remarks by Garis Robertson, the mayor of Burley, and by General James Brooks, chief of staff of the Idaho National Guard, the audience stood in silent tribute as the names were read of those from the community who had given their lives in the Vietnam War. This was a solemn and reflective moment.

One of the things I had missed most in prison was the customary celebration of Christmas. I had determined that after being released, whatever season of the year it was, I would have a little Christmas celebration with my loved ones, complete with a Christmas tree. Knowing of this wish of mine, my parents had arranged a family "Christmas party" on March 7, the day I arrived back in Burley with my children. There was the turkey and trimmings, the Christmas tree in its tinseled splendor, and its carpet of my gift-wrapped Christmas presents from family members. Best of all, we had had a joyous, wonderful family reunion.

Now, here in the school gymnasium these wonderful people of Burley, my larger "family," gave me another "little party"—twenty-five hundred people, a twelve-foot Christmas tree, a choir singing Christmas songs, and finally Santa Claus, who explained that "they don't like old Santa much over there in North Vietnam," so he couldn't visit me there because he "didn't want to get a reindeer shot down."

I had dreamed in prison about my homecoming, but Burley's welcome outdistanced any possible imaginings by a million miles. By the time I stood up to speak that afternoon in the gym, my heart was filled to overflowing with gratitude and warmth of feeling. I had said earlier to one of my friends, "Bill, I don't know what I'm going to say." "Don't worry about it, Larry," he replied. "As long as it comes from the heart it doesn't matter."

What I said in those emotion-packed remarks certainly came from the heart. I told those good peple something of my experiences as a POW, which I am sure they had come to hear. I truly felt that it was my obligation to repay them in some small way, if I could, for their doing so much for me. I bore my testimony of the gospel and tried to share with them the patriotic feelings we POWs had felt throughout our sojourn in prison. I thanked them for the warmth and love they had shown to my family and me. I hope that when I finished they knew of my love and appreciation for them.

MRS. CHESLEY AND SON LARRY IN A MOVING
MOMENT AS WELL-WISHER CALLS

—Church News photos, J. M. Heslop, photographer

STAR WARD SACRAMENT MEETING, BURLEY, IDAHO,
MARCH 11, 1973

In Star Ward, my parents' home ward, the next day I was privileged to speak in sacrament meeting. Again there was that warmth of feeling, the clear vibrations of love between myself and the audience. Over nine hundred people were present, some having been unable to stay for lack of seating accommodation or parking space. I was humbled by this tremendous turnout, and I prayed earnestly that the Lord would give me the words to say to that large group of both LDS and non-LDS people assembled in his house. His Spirit seemed indeed to be poured out upon that meeting.

The uniting of an entire community in a spontaneous expression of appreciation and welcome is something I shall never forget. It transcended denominational bounds—LDS and non-LDS were equally kind and concerned. Shortly after I arrived in Burley, Albert Klink came to our home. "I'm not LDS, as you know," he said to me, "but I prayed for you. And we prayed in our church for you." And I know they did. Prayers ascended daily on my behalf from all over that wonderful little community, and I know that they were answered.

"You just can't know how happy we are at your coming home," one good man said to me. But I could tell, I could tell it in their faces. It was genuine and sincere. The crowds came to see me because they really cared about me. Even people who did not know me before I was a prisoner cared about me and prayed for me. So that their little ones would know whom they had been praying for, parents brought children to see me who had not even been born when I was shot down. They saw in my homecoming an answer to their prayers, and it all showed in their faces.

In all this warm welcome I felt that I was really a symbol, a representative of a group of men who had done their best to keep faith—with God, with country, with the American people. The turnout to the welcoming celebrations was the ordinary person's way of silently whispering to all of us, "Thank you, thank you for what you have done for your country." That made the experience all the more

—*Church News photo, J. M. Heslop, photographer*

AUTHOR RELAXES WITH HIS CHILDREN

humbling, because the POWs generally felt that we did only what we were supposed to do for our country, only what others would have done if they had found themselves in our circumstances. When I expressed this thought, people would say: "Well, yes, maybe others would have done it but you *did* do it, and that's the important thing." However that might be, to me I was the symbol. That was why my community was honoring me.

As well as doing this in person, people phoned and sent cards by the hundreds and letters by the thousands. Most of them didn't even know me—they knew only my name from a POW bracelet and that I had been a prisoner of war, and they wanted to express their appreciation and wish me well. To one like me who was raised in humble circumstances with no pretensions to being a celebrity it was all a very humbling experience.

Many people in this country wore a metal bracelet stamped with a particular POW's name, not removing it from the wrist until that POW arrived home. Connie Rae Lytle, an eighth-grade teacher at the Robert Stuart Junior High School in Twin Falls, Idaho, had written to my parents saying that she was wearing my bracelet. After I returned she had her students write me letters and cards. One of the letters she sent was forty feet long, and on it each of her students had written a letter to me.

I called Connie Lytle and told her I would like to come and thank the kids personally. So I went to Twin Falls. The school had been named after Robert Stuart, a pioneer of Magic Valley. I found a wonderful spirit among the youth in that school, and I was happy and proud to be associated with them.

Perhaps the welcome that affected my soul most deeply was the quiet one I received in a home in Burley—the home of Alfred Knight, the man who in 1955 gave me the patriarchal blessing on which my parents and I, though separated by thousands of miles and the gulf of uncertainty, had pinned our hopes during the hard prison years. He had been ailing for some time—in fact when my parents received the news early in February 1973 that I was coming home, he was in the hospital very ill. My father went to visit him.

At the hospital his son said, "Father's not very well to-night, Bishop Chesley, but you just go on in and see him." When my father walked into the room, Mrs. Knight said, "Bishop Chesley, Alfred's not coherent, but you might talk to him." And turning toward the bed, she said, "Alfred, there's a visitor here to see you."

My father walked over and looked the sick man right in the eyes. He spoke slowly. "Brother Knight, this is Bishop Chesley. Larry has been released. I'm going to pick up my son, Brother Knight."

Brother Knight comprehended. "Bishop Chesley," he asked, "how long has it been since I told that boy he'd come home? Twenty years?" He was now rational and clear-headed.

"Yes, Brother Knight," Dad responded, "it's been nearly twenty years."

"I knew he'd come home," said the man in the bed. "I knew he was a good boy."

When I went back to Burley, of course I went to see Brother Knight. He was now home from the hospital and a little better. There were tears in his eyes as he spoke.

"I prayed for you, Larry. I knew you would come home."

"Brother Knight," I replied, "if I'm any judge of myself I knew that I was keeping my part of the bargain; and I knew that if I kept my part God would keep his. I didn't think it would take this long. But in the blessing it says 'wherever you go you shall be watched over,' and I know that the Lord did keep his part of the bargain."

The Lord keeps his part of the bargain with all of us. Of the many things I learned in North Vietnam, nothing is more significant than that.

Chapter 12

OF WHITEWASH
AND HOGWASH

It was inevitable that as the POWs began to arrive back in the United States news reports would flood the nation with their comments on the conditions they had experienced in North Vietnam. In order not to give provocation for the maltreatment or delayed repatriation of any still in captivity, the returned prisoners' comments were deliberately restrained until the last known prisoner was safely back on U.S. soil. We knew better than anyone else that none of those remaining were entirely safe from the cruelty of their captors until they were securely in U.S. hands. When the last known prisoner was out "the lid was off" and the true picture of life in the North Vietnamese prison camps began to emerge from news conferences held with returned POWs across the nation.

If this pattern was inevitable, it was equally certain that the North Vietnamese government would seek to counter these developments by declarations of innocence. Accordingly they have issued statements reiterating the position they maintained to the outside world for the entire period of 8½ years from the time they captured the first American flyer in August 1964 until the last one was released in March

1973. That position is that at all times the prisoners received humane and lenient treatment.

Of course they have specifically denied that any prisoner was tortured, and this despite the testimonies of the many men who have revealed the beatings and other torments which the prison authorities deliberately inflicted upon them. As an example, an Associated Press dispatch reported in the *Salt Lake Tribune* of April 2, 1973, paraphrases the North Vietnamese official communist party newspaper *Nhan Dan* as saying that "returning prisoners' torture stories were drummed up to deflect attention from U.S. 'crimes' in Vietnam." It goes on to quote verbatim from the official Vietnam News Agency broadcast of the *Nhan Dan* commentary:

"The pilots of U.S. piratic planes who bombed during the last eight years were criminals. However, in keeping with their humanitarian policy and for the sake of their friendship with the American people, the government and the Vietnamese people treated them well."

North Vietnamese efforts to support the "humanitarian" image are apparent in an interview given to an AP reporter at Hanoi Hilton the day after the last American prisoners left that camp. The thousand-word report, carried in the *Salt Lake Tribune* of March 18, 1973, capsules a "guided tour" of the camp which was conducted by the "smiling, chain-smoking camp commander, Captain Truong Son." The description makes me think of the genial photographic portrayals I have seen of "Uncle Joe Stalin," whose gross and gigantic crimes against humanity are common knowledge. Communists, it seems, can torture and kill—and then go home smiling to dinner and a good night's sleep.

While the camp commander's attempts to mislead would be immediately obvious to any former POW occupant of Hanoi Hilton, the American public are not in a position to evaluate this or similar articles on North Vietnamese statements about prison conditions. It may help if I quote from the article and make a few observations.

The article begins: "Pieces of dirty prison clothes, a pile of well-read books, some graffiti and memories were all that was left Saturday of American war prisoners at the Hanoi Hilton." As to "pieces of dirty prison clothes," I have explained earlier that when our group left Hanoi Hilton we put all of our old clothing in boxes, stacked them up neatly, and swept and cleaned the room as well as we possibly could with the materials the camp authorities gave us. Our senior officers gave this instruction to all groups, and I'm sure they all followed these orders.

The "well-read" books would certainly have been very much in evidence. In late January and early February of 1973 the prison authorities at Hanoi Hilton finally let us have a few of the magazines that had been arriving for us for the previous seven years or so. You bet they were well read! We pounced on them, we devoured them, we were so desperately anxious to get something to read other than North Vietnamese propaganda. Yes, I can believe there was a pile of well-read books in each of the rooms. Since the last man left in about mid-March, the magazines were available to POWs at Hanoi Hilton for a total of four to six weeks. The long years before that—nothing!

"Whitewashed cell blocks." Well, they did whitewash the rooms once in the seven years I was in and out of Hanoi Hilton.

"POWs slept on elevated concrete blocks covered with wooden boards and rattan mats." True—except that sometimes there were no boards. We used folded clothing for a pillow. Every thirty minutes or so during the night the sleeper had to turn over to relieve pressure on the shoulders and hips.

"Fifteen to thirty American POWs in each cell block." In our large room originally there were fifty-seven, giving us seventeen inches of space apiece to sleep in. When the number dropped to forty-eight, I believe that gave us twenty-one inches each to sleep in. Thirty in one of those rooms would have given reasonable sleeping space—for prisoners. Fifteen would have represented luxurious sleeping arrangements, though we in any case preferred to have more in the rooms so that we could live as closer-knit units. This preference of ours of course had nothing to do with the living arrangements.

"Guards tended grapevines and some rose bushes in the courtyard between the prison gate and the drab prisoners' compound." It would have been entertaining to see the guards I knew enacting this touching pastoral scene. Of course, the vines and roses weren't there all the time—only for such purposes as photos taken to send to the Red Cross or to put on a show for visitors. In any case, we couldn't normally see them when they were there, penned up as we were continually in our little cells or partitioned courtyards—unless we happened to be able to peek out from under a blindfold when moving to or from Hanoi Hilton.

As we know, Hanoi Hilton was built by the French to house Vietnamese prisoners. The article reports Capt. Son: "When we decided to use the prison for the Americans we worked hard to improve it. We broke down many walls to make much bigger cells. We had no solitary for the Americans."

This is actually the reverse of the truth. The big rooms we lived in at Camp Unity were typical of all the rooms at Hanoi Hilton until the prison authorities, having discovered the significance of our five-by-five block of letters, decided they would try to break up our communication with one another. They then built the small cells in Little Vegas that I described in chapter 4, making hallways between the rooms. Far from breaking down walls to make rooms bigger, they erected walls to make rooms smaller, and the plaster on those walls was still wet when we POWs were put in there in February 1967. It's another lie when they say they had no solitary for Americans there. Solitary cells were built by the North Vietnamese to house American POWs, and some of our men lived alone in them for over four years.

"We flattened the courtyard so that our prisoners could play volleyball and basketball and we built them a club to play bridge, Ping Pong and chess." I can't swear that they didn't build a prisoners' club somewhere in January or February 1973, but I've never heard of one. I can only speak of where I was, and certainly there was no bridge or other club at Hanoi Hilton or any other camp I was ever in. It is true, though, that they let us play Ping Pong, volleyball and basketball—for the last twenty days I was in captivity. Twenty days out of twenty-five hundred!

Pictures have been released of POWs playing basketball and volleyball and so forth. It's true that a few prisoners were allowed to do that, but until the last month or so they were in a very small minority. In my rooms we were allowed to play volleyball one time in the first 6½ years I was there. It was a Vietnamese holiday. The guards were playing volleyball and a group of us POWs were allowed out of our small courtyard to sweep the yard as they played. When they had finished their game, we just sort of moved in and started playing. Strangely, they didn't stop us.

As to special courtyard facilities, in the first place we didn't even get outside to a courtyard for more than about fifteen minutes at a time at irregular intervals (to sweep the yard, for example) until November 1970. Even so, the outside area in which they would let us maneuver was too small to exercise in, so we would exercise on our bunks and by running around the big rooms, close quarters as it was. We did our exercising right inside the room. This was true too in the earlier days in the smaller rooms, when in any case we were not allowed outside.

"When we learned about American habits and customs we built a fireplace and a barbeque pit—so that our prisoners could prepare their food the American way." Where, I wonder? As with the bridge club, they must have kept this fireplace and pit well hidden. As for preparing our own food (imagine barbecued pumpkin soup!) the extent of that preparation was to peel a few vegetables when we were in the camp near the Chinese border. In that camp too they gave us a bucket with the side partly cut out and a little wood. This was the "fireplace" (no barbecue pit!) we used to heat water for the guys to make coffee.

"When it was hot during the summer months we gave them an electric fan for each cell. Then we organized a broadcast system with two or three loudspeakers in each room." It's true that in the summer of 1971 they put one fan in our sixty-foot by twenty-four-foot room. And it helped to keep us a little cooler in that hot sultry weather. But they could have helped us much better by forgetting about a fan and merely removing the mats covering the three south windows. We had two loudspeakers in our room too—unfortunately. Their quality was so terrible that even if you had wanted to listen you could barely make out what was being said.

The camp commander continues: "In the daytime the prisoners could stay in the courtyard and do what they liked." For the final twenty days of my captivity we were allowed out of our room most of the day. The tarpaper partitions which had until now sectioned off the courtyard to make a small self contained area per cell block were torn down, and we could now circulate in the large compound. Now for the first time we could use the large courtyard to visit with POWs from other buildings, play games, do small jobs, clean and prepare food, clean our rooms, and so on. It's true that for twenty days of my entire period of captivity "in the daytime the prisoners could stay in the courtyard and do [very largely] what they liked."

No doubt with tongue in cheek, the AP writer referred to the camp commander and his military interpreters beaming as they recited "numerous other amenities of the Hilton, like efficient public relations managers." In some ways that's an apt description. With the POWs as their public, they managed relations with us very efficiently. They would beat or torture us until we did what they wanted. I guess that's pretty efficient.

"Of course each prisoner could complain, and every day the prisoners had a chance to contact a North Vietnamese officer, but we never received one complaint. I think they realized that they got fair treatment." We did have a chance to complain sometimes—now and again, toward the end. And we did complain, but it didn't do any good. We asked for better conditions but they didn't give them to us. "I think they realize that they got fair treatment" said the camp commander. No prisoner received fair treatment over there. Absolutely not one.

A guard explained to the reporter the reasons for a blackboard at the end of a cell. "That is for the Americans that were willing to learn." Willing to learn! We were so eager that we'd have given our eye teeth for real opportunities to learn. With nothing to do we made up things to do, we taught each other, we learned from each other about anything and everything anyone knew, however lacking in practical value that knowledge might be to most of us in normal life. What the guard probably meant was, willing to learn the propaganda and lies they tried to feed us. I believe one room in our block did have a blackboard for a week or two at the end. No room I was ever in had one.

"In the center of the courtyard there is a wooden thatched-roof shack that served as a reading room. Two small cubicles were reserved for opening mail from home." Yes, there's a wooden shack in the middle of the courtyard. It's a reading room. Yes, it's a real reading room—for reading the propaganda garbage they put out for us to read. And the two little cubicles reserved for us for opening mail from home? That's right. They allowed my first letter through $4\frac{1}{2}$ years after I was captured. I opened it, got to read it in the special cubicle for five minutes, and then had to give it back. I never saw it again until two days before leaving Hanoi, when all my letters were returned to me. It was the same for every POW—about four times a year we got a six-line letter, and this was the procedure for reading them. As the prison authorities say, we got to read our letters in special cubicles.

The "prisoners' kitchen"? Sounds nice—getting out of those cells for a while each day. We did do some KP—during the last twenty days we were there. Never before that in Hanoi Hilton.

"A small wooden hut was the dispensary where, according to the camp commander, prisoners could get all medicines needed to cure minor ailments." Yes, there was a dispensary. Getting "all medicines needed to cure minor ailments" was something else again. Many times a man would go for days and weeks, needing only some Merthiolate or Mercurochrome or iodine, but the camp authorities wouldn't give it to us. Almost never would they give us even aspirin to relieve a bad headache.

An example of this was when I broke out in boils. Many men had boils. They may have been caused by the radical change of diet, or sometimes by infection, or simply by not being able to keep clean. The camp authorities would not give me some penicillin or other medication to try to kill the virus. Sometimes they would clean the boils eventually, after they had burst—put some sulpha or something in them to make them heal. Frequently they did nothing at all when a man had boils. The boils just had to get better on their own.

One fellow had bad teeth, infection in his mouth, and I suspect that this is what caused him to keep breaking out in boils. In the early days of captivity men with bad teeth suffered severely. This kind of pressure was just what our captors wanted. They would tell a man he could have his teeth taken care of if he would write a statement denouncing the U.S. government, or one to be used at the Betrand Russell Tribunal, or some other propaganda statement. The man of course would refuse, so he didn't get his teeth taken care of. (Even if he *had* written as suggested, he probably wouldn't have received the dental treatment.) To the sufferer this could be torture in itself, as everyone knows who has ever had a toothache.

I had a similar experience myself in February 1967, shortly after my return from Briarpatch to Hanoi Hilton. I was taken to a "quiz," as we called the interrogations which preceded torture, by the officer we knew as Rabbit. This was during the period of intense pain in my feet caused by beriberi, which I referred to in chapter 3.

My extremity was Rabbit's opportunity, so he came up with an interesting proposition: Write this statement or we'll hurt your feet. The continuous pain and the associated depression of spirit perhaps made me more than usually resentful of the camp authorities and their treatment, and I responded with some vigor: "Look, there's no way you can hurt my feet worse than they're hurting right now, so do what you like." It turned out to be a try-on, an attempt to get a statement by threat alone. When it didn't work I was sent back to my cell.

After October 1969, when conditions began to get a little better, the Vietnamese did have their dentists work on some men's teeth. They pulled a few teeth, drilled some and put in fillings. The fillings usually would not last more than a week, often less. Most of them got knocked out by the small white rocks in the rice we were served. I'm sure these rocks, which looked just like rice, were not put there intentionally; it was just that the rice wasn't cleaned very well. You had to be very careful because you could really bang your teeth up in eating rice.

We had men that were sick, as I was, for most of the time they were in prison. If a man got very seriously ill, the Vietnamese would usually take care of him. But if a man was able to walk and breathe he was by definition fit enough and required no medical attention. As a result of this neglect, some of the injured men have come home with withered arms and legs, open wounds, scars, etc. A few have come back with pins in their legs or arms, etc.; they came out of it okay because they were taken care of in time. But these are a very small minority and their captivity extended over only the later years.

The North Vietnamese have given out that they gave us immunization shots. My recollection is that we received three in seven years—one shot at three different times in a seven-year period. These were supposed to immunize us against typhoid, tetanus, and several other diseases, which one shot of the size we received could not possibly do.

The thing that probably did us the most good as far as medical aid was concerned was the vitamins our families sent in our packages. The North Vietnamese did let us have these vitamins. They almost totally eliminated colds for me. I'm a big believer in vitamins now.

The last statement in the AP article quotes a prison officer in words that still try to preserve the fiction of humane treatment. "We were only concerned with giving [the POWs] fair treatment," he said. In truth, they were not concerned with giving us anything. The only good things they did for us, few as they were, were done for propaganda value. They even treated our families inhumanely by withholding captives' names so that back home they didn't know whether the men were dead or alive.

No doubt unconvinced by the impressive "public relations" effort mounted at Hanoi Hilton, the reporter makes a simple yet true comment on the camp commander's affirmations about fair treatment. He writes: "Only the prisoners can finally tell what really happened at the Hanoi Hilton, what it was really like."

I go along with that.

Chapter 13

GOD BLESS AMERICA

Now that it's all behind me and I've returned to "normal" living again, I find there are some adjustments to be made. America has changed a little since 1966.

Fashion is one area of change. Women's skirts are much shorter, men's hair much longer. No doubt both these trends will pass—whether phasing into something better or worse, only time and good judgment will tell. As to the hair style, in prison one of the fellows received a photo showing his boy with very long hair. Concerned, he wrote back to his wife about it. I thought her reply very appropriate: "Don't worry about the long hair, worry about how they are doing academically. Your kids are all number one in their classes. Worry about how they are doing in sports and in music. They are doing very well in these areas too. Don't worry about the long hair. It's a fad; it will pass in a few years."

The fashion changes in men's clothes may be even less significant. I don't suppose wearing double-knit red trousers, a red check shirt and a six-inch wide tie will keep a man out of heaven. Despite my normally conservative tastes, then, I decided that beating 'em was impossible so I'd better join 'em. While I was at Travis I went to a store with someone else and asked him to pick out some clothes for me—I'd wear them, I told him, whether I liked them or not.

Naturally we POWs were not entirely unaware, during the latter part of our captivity, of the changes that had taken place in America. As the B-52 bombings stepped up, captured crews from these aircraft brought news of the outside world which, now that we were in larger rooms and had somewhat easier communication from room to room, was passed around among us. Some of the developments I heard about in this way gave me concern. None gave me more uneasiness of mind than the so-called "sexual revolution."

I got my first taste of this trend before I even left Vietnamese airspace. Our plane had just gotten airborne from Gia Lam airport when magazines were passed out to us. How great to get a current U.S. magazine in my hands again! was my first thought. Seconds later I wasn't so sure. I opened the magazine and the first picture I saw was, to me, pornographic beyond description. I couldn't believe it! I hadn't seen even an artist's drawing of such a thing in any magazine before 1966, whereas here was an actual photograph of a girl and a guy in a very ugly position. I tossed the magazine aside in disgust. This wasn't a part of the America I knew and loved. Whether I even wanted to "adjust" to this kind of thing, I didn't know.

My concern on this point has not diminished since then, nor have my views changed one bit from those I held in prison. To me, moral cleanliness is still not only indispensable to happy living and to a decent society but is inseparable from true religion. Whatever their apologists may say, filthy books, pictures and movies befoul the mind and the soul and motivate to an unclean life. This in turn undermines character and destroys the moral fibre of the individual, the family, and the nation. The drug kick is working in the same direction.

It's easy to see that these and other bad developments naturally impinge more upon our youth than on others. Shortly after I arrived back in the Intermountain area I was privileged and honored to have an interview with President Harold B. Lee. During our conversation he referred particularly to the problems and temptations that confront youth today, and told me that this is one of the foremost concerns of the Church. It was obvious that he has a special love for the youth of the Church and is anxious that they preserve the Lord's code of morals and other basic commandments in their lives and thus enjoy the happiness that is their birthright.

I no doubt lost a lot by my seven years' captivity, but I like to think it wasn't all loss. I believe I learned a thing or two there and reaffirmed others. One thing I learned was the futility of worrying over something one can't control.

Worry lived with most of us in prison. Of the many things I worried about, my broken back was high on the list. I worried about it for nearly seven years. After about the first nine to twelve months it didn't hurt any more and I could do everything with it I could do before, but I was still worried. I knew that it had been injured quite severely and thought that when I got back to the States I would need an operation and that would put me back in prison—the prison of a hospital and a body cast of some kind. I hated the thought of those forthcoming days.

When I got to the hospital at Travis AFB the doctor who examined me told me that everything was okay, that my back had healed itself. Calcium had built up the bone and healed the fracture. After seven years of worrying about it there had been nothing to worry about!

In the entire time, the only treatment I received for my back was a shot to deaden the pain a few days after the vertebra broke. You may be sure I prayed a lot about the matter. In the early days in prison I had a muscle running down the right side of my back that was almost as big as my forearm. I assume it was acting as a brace. My body twisted enough to hold my back straight. My left shoulder is now about two inches higher and two inches further forward than my right shoulder and my left leg is twisted to the left. The point is that with the Lord's blessing, my back healed. The worry was all unnecessary.

I've mentioned earlier another thing I came to realize in prison—the value of learning. I plan to read and study the kind and quantity of books I hungered for in North Vietnam.

In prison I believe I learned something about gratitude, especially appreciation for the "little" things in life. I'm thinking of things like soap and toothpaste that we naturally take for granted in America. There were times when we didn't have such things in prison. It's hard to imagine how filthy and uncomfortable you can get if you don't have any toilet paper for days or weeks and can't bathe. And hot water to wash in? Seven years without hot water can do a lot to stir a sense of appreciation for what little things you *can* get.

Gratitude is something it is pretty hard not to have in prison. Virtually all the POWs were grateful for the little things we did have. When we got well after being sick, we were more grateful than I can express. We didn't complain so much about being in prison, because at least now we were healthy and felt strong again, and that was more basic there than elsewhere since we couldn't get medical aid. And we were deeply thankful for each other, thankful that we had a strong feeling of friendship and brotherhood.

I believe I've learned something about service too. I'm thinking particularly about service to God through service to his children. Foolishly I didn't go on a mission for the Church. At the time I passed up this honor of serving God I didn't regret it, but I certainly do now. Aside from the blessing it could have been to others, which is the most important factor, those two years would have brought me greater strength and maturity. I hope to serve diligently in the Church for the rest of my life, including a two-year mission at some time in the future.

As to my military service, I have no regrets about spending those years serving my country. I believe that any young man living in America should be willing to serve this country in the military if called upon to do so. To me, this land is blessed of the Lord above all other lands even in a material sense, as I observe just from my own travels in Europe and the Far East. The most modest income here will secure luxuries unknown to the rich in many parts of the world.

More important is the American concept of freedom, a concept reaffirmed in prison by the POW's memories of home, the comments shared with his comrades, the contrasting philosophy and behavior of his captors, and that indefinable inner urge which is the heritage of every free man. We knew in prison of the "peace" marches in the States, the burnings of the American flag, the riotous voices of dissent complete with the display of the enemy's flag, the visits to North Vietnam of U.S. citizens sympathetic to the enemy—being favorable to the enemy's cause and unfavorable to ours, such developments were pounded into us by their propaganda machine. It was discouraging in our circumstances and filled us with disgust, but it did not deflect our hearts from the ideal of freedom.

We managed to reconcile ourselves to all this with the thought that as servicemen it was our duty to fight for America's freedoms, among which is the right to dissent. We might disagree with the dissenters. We might consider them ill-advised, immature, blind to reality. We might wish for them the experience of living for a few years in North Vietnam and trying to show their dissent there by protest marches and by flying the American flag. But still it was our responsibility as necessary to protect their right to act wrong.

Our coming back to the States corrected or shifted the emphasis, it would seem. It showed me that there are still many fine people in this land who respond to patriotic urges. Many people have told me that the POWs' return was for the nation a tremendous event even more moving than the TV pictures of Neil Armstrong stepping onto the moon. That first moon-walk happened a few years ago, of course, and memories dim with time. But it does seem from what people have told me that our coming home was good for the American people, pulling them together a little. There had naturally been divisions of opinion over the Vietnam War, and perhaps

—*Times News, Twin Falls, Idaho, photo,*
David Horseman, photographer

CAPTAIN CHESLEY WITH PARENTS AND CHILDREN
ON REVIEWING STAND DURING BURLEY PARADE,
MARCH 10, 1973

the returning prisoners have represented a common bond,
and by identifying with them Americans have felt and expressed a deepening of love and appreciation for our great
country and all it means to us. This has been made easier
by the fact that, although apparently there were those who
thought that the returning POWs would come back embit-
tered by their long imprisonment, almost to a man we have
come back with our heads high praising our country and our
leaders.

Like the first moon landing, the memory of the POWs'
return will fade from public recollection. The men themselves

will not forget so quickly. Memory being blessedly constituted, it seems, to screen out the unpleasant and zoom in on the happier facets of the past, we will undoubtedly relive much oftener the joyous, emotion-packed welcome given us by our brother Americans than the maltreatment and cruelty of our Vietnamese captors. For me, there will always be a vivid reminder in the Associated Press picture which appeared on the front pages of most of the largest newspapers in America, showing me in the bus at Clark AFB, my thumbs up and my face showing the feelings of my heart—profound joy at being home, gladness at having come through it all with basic health apparently unimpaired, deep gratitude to the American people and government who cared about us.

In conclusion, while with the other former POWs I hold the spotlight for this brief moment, before the lights dim and others move to center stage, let me briefly recall the great reaffirmation I experienced in my prison years. It is that, however tough the going gets, God never deserts us if we put our trust in him and try to do his will. It is that under God's blessing the United States of America is the greatest country on the earth. It is that God and America is the great latter-day combination for man's freedom and happiness—if the American people will but do the right and put their trust in God.

God and country—that is the great combination. Navy Cmdr. Jeremiah Denton said it at the end of the short speech representative of us all which he gave as he stepped off the first plane from Hanoi. The military newspaper *Stars and Stripes* picked it up and headlined it "Three Words Say It All." With all my heart I reiterate those three words, with a prayer that the American people will increasingly comprehend the true implications of those words and live for their fulfillment.

GOD BLESS AMERICA